11.14.18
$47.99

Withdrawn

To:

....

From:

....

Date:

....

GOD'S GOOD NEWS

Billy Graham

ILLUSTRATED BY Scott Wakefield

MORE THAN

60 BIBLE

STORIES &
DEVOTIONS

Tommy
NELSON

An Imprint of Thomas Nelson

God's Good News

© 2015, 2018 by Billy Graham

Previously published as *God's Good News Bible Storybook*

Published in Nashville, Tennessee, by Tommy Nelson. Tommy Nelson is an imprint of Thomas Nelson. Thomas Nelson is a registered trademark of HarperCollins Christian Publishing, Inc.

Illustrated by Scott Wakefield

This text includes material that has been adapted from previously published works by Billy Graham and is used with his permission.
Angels: God's Secret Agents (Nashville: Nelson, 1995)
Answers to Life's Problems (Nashville: Nelson, 1994)
The Billy Graham Training Center Bible (Nashville: Nelson, 2004)
How to Be Born Again (Nashville: Nelson, 1989)
The Holy Spirit (Nashville: Nelson, 1988)
Hope for Each Day: Morning and Evening Devotions (Nashville: Nelson, 2012)
Hope for the Troubled Heart (Nashville: Nelson, 1993)
Peace with God (Nashville: Nelson, 1997)
The Journey: How to Live by Faith in an Uncertain World (Nashville: Nelson, 2006)
The Reason for My Hope: Salvation (Nashville: Nelson, 2013)
Unto the Hills: A Daily Devotional (Nashville: Nelson, 1996)
Wisdom for Each Day (Nashville: Nelson, 2008)
Selections from "My Answer" column (1993, 1994)

This text also includes material that has been adapted from sermons delivered by Billy Graham and is used with his permission.
"The Grace of God," 1954
Sermon on Exodus 2 at Greater London Crusade, 1954
"Choice," 1957
"Don't Be Like Samson," 1957
"Battle of the Giants," 1968
"John the Baptist"
Salute to Automobile Companies, 1979
"Filthy Rich," 1982
"Joseph," 1997
Prayer of Invocation at Special Olympics, 1999

Tommy Nelson titles may be purchased in bulk for educational, business, fund-raising, or sales promotional use. For information, please e-mail SpecialMarkets@ThomasNelson.com.

Scripture quotations are taken from the New King James Version®. © 1982 by Thomas Nelson. Used by permission. All rights reserved.

Bible stories are a combination of paraphrased Bible text, which appears in italics, and actual Bible text that has been extracted to be readable and accessible to young readers.

ISBN: 978-1-4002-0989-7

Library of Congress Cataloging-in-Publication Data is on file.

Printed in China

18 19 20 21 22 DSC 6 5 4 3 2 1

Jesus called them to Him and said,
"Let the little children come to Me, and do not forbid them;
for of such is the kingdom of God."

—LUKE 18:16

The Old Testament

The New Testament

Dear Reader,

As a boy my idea of the ocean was so small that the first time I saw the Atlantic I couldn't comprehend that any little lake could be so big! The vastness of the ocean cannot be understood until it is seen.

This is the same with God's love. It passes knowledge. Until you actually experience it, no one can describe its wonders to you.

In your hands you hold stories—amazing stories—from the Bible, the Word of God. These are not stories someone made up; they actually happened! They tell about real people and real events. Those who witnessed what happened wrote it down so people like you and me could know all about it. It's clear: God wants *you* to know these stories. Why?

These stories will help you understand God's good news—the news that God has a plan for your life, that God loves you, and that He is a God of mercy. He will forgive you, lead you, and bless you if you confess and turn away from your sins and trust Jesus Christ as your personal Savior and Lord. These stories will point you to the most important event in history: the life, death, and resurrection of Jesus Christ. "God so loved the world that He gave His only begotten Son, that whoever believes in Him should not perish but have everlasting life" (John 3:16). This is the greatest news in the universe!

They will also show you God's wonderful way of living—loving Him and loving others. He wants to show you who He is and help you be like Him. And this can happen because God doesn't leave you to do it alone! He wants to be with you every step of the way, guiding and helping you, because He loves you and wants what is best for you.

My prayer for you as you read this book is that God will use it to help you begin a new journey with Him—the greatest, most exciting journey you could ever experience. As we'll see from the people in these stories, it isn't always an easy journey. But even in the midst of problems and troubles, you can have strength and joy when God is with you. Most of all, it is a journey of hope, because it leads us to heaven.

No matter how young you are, I invite you to explore this journey for yourself. May God bless you as you read this book and teach you through its pages how you, along with so many believers before you, can live out God's good news—following Him every day, and receiving His love and passing it on to others.

The Old Testament

God Created . . . Everything!

Day and Night, Earth and Seas

Selected Scripture from Genesis 1

In the beginning God created the heavens and the earth. Then God said, "Let there be light"; and there was light. God called the light Day, and the darkness He called Night. So the evening and the morning were the first day.

God made the firmament and divided the waters under the firmament from the waters above the firmament; and it was so. And God called the firmament Heaven. So the evening and the morning were the second day.

Then God said, "Let the waters be gathered together into one place, and let the dry land appear"; and it was so. And God called the dry land Earth, and the gathering of the waters He called Seas. And God saw that it was good.

Then God said, "Let the earth bring forth grass, the herb that yields seed, and the fruit tree that yields fruit"; and it was so. So the evening and the morning were the third day.

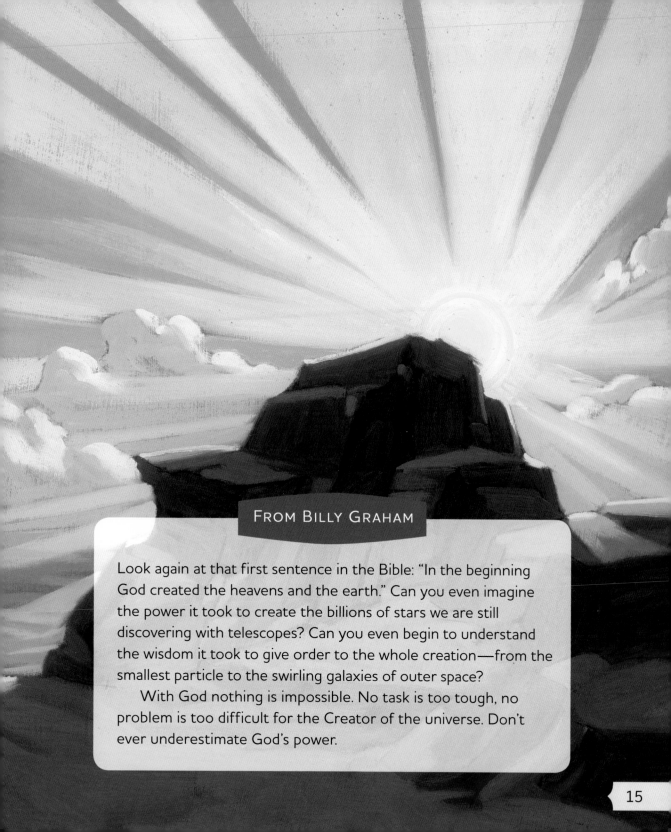

FROM BILLY GRAHAM

Look again at that first sentence in the Bible: "In the beginning God created the heavens and the earth." Can you even imagine the power it took to create the billions of stars we are still discovering with telescopes? Can you even begin to understand the wisdom it took to give order to the whole creation—from the smallest particle to the swirling galaxies of outer space?

With God nothing is impossible. No task is too tough, no problem is too difficult for the Creator of the universe. Don't ever underestimate God's power.

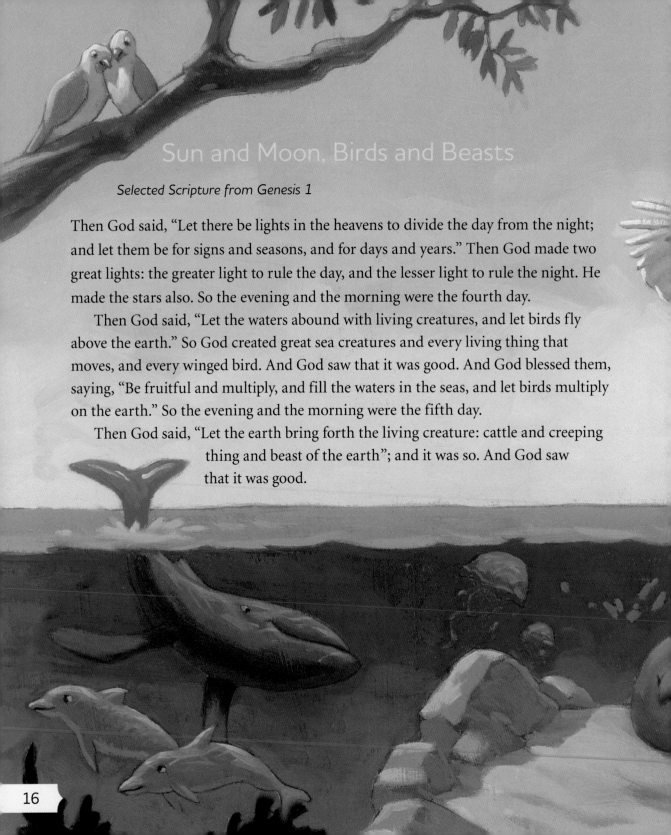

Sun and Moon, Birds and Beasts

Selected Scripture from Genesis 1

Then God said, "Let there be lights in the heavens to divide the day from the night; and let them be for signs and seasons, and for days and years." Then God made two great lights: the greater light to rule the day, and the lesser light to rule the night. He made the stars also. So the evening and the morning were the fourth day.

Then God said, "Let the waters abound with living creatures, and let birds fly above the earth." So God created great sea creatures and every living thing that moves, and every winged bird. And God saw that it was good. And God blessed them, saying, "Be fruitful and multiply, and fill the waters in the seas, and let birds multiply on the earth." So the evening and the morning were the fifth day.

Then God said, "Let the earth bring forth the living creature: cattle and creeping thing and beast of the earth"; and it was so. And God saw that it was good.

Adam and Eve

Selected Scripture from Genesis 1–2

Then God said, "Let Us make man in Our image, according to Our likeness; let them have dominion over the fish of the sea, over the birds of the air, and over the cattle, over all the earth and over every creeping thing on the earth." So God created man in His own image; in the image of God He created him; male and female He created them. Then God blessed them, and God said to them, "Be fruitful and multiply; fill the earth and subdue it; have dominion over the fish of the sea, over the birds of the air, and over every living thing that moves on the earth."

Then God saw everything that He had made, and indeed it was very good. So the evening and the morning were the sixth day.

And on the seventh day God ended His work, and He rested on the seventh day from all His work. Then God blessed the seventh day and sanctified it, because in it He rested from all His work.

FROM BILLY GRAHAM

Do you know why God made you? It is the greatest discovery you will ever make: you were created to know God and to be His friend forever.

We were not made for ourselves; we were made for God. We are not here by accident; we are here because God put us here—and He put us here so we could know Him and love Him. God wants you to be His friend!

The First Sin

Selected Scripture from Genesis 2–3

God took the man and put him in the garden of Eden to tend and keep it. [He said,] "Of every tree of the garden you may freely eat; but of the tree of the knowledge of good and evil you shall not eat."

When Eve came to the garden, the serpent told her that they should not believe what God said. So Eve disobeyed God by eating the fruit; then Adam did the same—and their lives changed forever. Ashamed, they hid from God. But He went to talk to them.

"Have you eaten from the tree of which I commanded you that you should not eat?"

The man said, "The woman whom You gave to be with me, she gave me of the tree, and I ate."

God said to the woman, "What is this you have done?"

The woman said, "The serpent deceived me, and I ate."

God made them clothes and sent them out of Eden.

Adam and Eve weren't robots. They were free to choose to love God but also free to choose not to love Him. If they had not been free, then their "love" for God wouldn't have been love at all, because we only truly love someone when we freely choose to love them. From their first moment on earth, they chose to love God.

But then something went terribly wrong. Adam and Eve rebelled against God. They did what they wanted to do, not what God wanted them to do.

What happened in Eden happens to us every day. We all are guilty of sin because we all choose our own way instead of God's way. But when we admit this to God and confess our sins, we take the first step toward choosing His way—the best way.

Noah and God's Rainbow Promise

Selected Scripture from Genesis 6–9

All the people on earth had forgotten about God and had become evil. But one man still followed God. His name was Noah. God told Noah to build an ark, and He gave Noah very specific building plans. God told Noah about a great flood to come and a great promise.

God said to Noah, "I will establish My covenant with you; and you shall go into the ark—you, your sons, your wife, and your sons' wives with you. And of every living thing you shall bring two into the ark; they shall be male and female. And you shall take for yourself food for you and for them."

Noah did according to all that God commanded him.

Then the LORD said to Noah, "Come into the ark, you and all your household, because I have seen that you are righteous before Me. For after seven days I will cause it to rain on the earth forty days and forty nights, and I will destroy all living things that I have made."

It came to pass after seven days that the waters of the flood were on the earth. All the fountains of the great deep were broken up, and the windows of heaven were opened.

Noah and Noah's sons, Shem, Ham, and Japheth, and Noah's wife and the three wives of his sons entered the ark—they and every beast and every bird. They went into the ark to Noah, two by two, male and female; and the LORD shut him in.

The flood was on the earth forty days. The waters increased and lifted up the ark, and it rose high above the earth. [God] destroyed all living things on the face of the ground: both man and cattle, creeping thing and bird of the air. Only Noah and those who were with him in the ark remained alive. And the waters prevailed on the earth one hundred and fifty days.

FROM BILLY GRAHAM

Can you imagine what the people thought when Noah began chopping down trees and building an enormous ark on dry land, far from any ocean? Noah knew nothing about sailing the high seas, and he certainly was at a loss as to how to build a boat, even with God's detailed instructions. But he believed God when He said it would rain and the land would flood, and Noah faithfully carried out God's command.

Building a huge boat on dry land made no sense to Noah's human understanding. But when he obeyed God, Noah showed that he trusted God, and God was pleased. Because of Noah's faith and obedience, God called Noah righteous and saved Noah, his family, and the animals.

Let us be as faithful as Noah was in the things God has called us to do!

Then God remembered Noah and made a wind to pass over the earth, and the waters subsided. The fountains of the deep and the windows of heaven were also stopped, and the rain from heaven was restrained.

At the end of forty days, Noah opened the window of the ark. He sent out a dove to see if the waters had receded from the ground. But the dove found no resting place, and she returned into the ark. He waited yet another seven days, and again he sent the dove out. Then the dove came to him in the evening, and a freshly plucked olive leaf was in her mouth; and Noah knew that the waters had receded.

Then God spoke to Noah and to his sons, saying: "As for Me, behold, I establish My covenant with you and with your descendants after you: Never again shall all flesh be cut off by the waters of the flood; never again shall there be a flood to destroy the earth.

"I set My rainbow in the cloud, and it shall be the sign of the covenant between Me and the earth."

Just imagine being aboard the ark in heavy rain for forty days, riding the gigantic waves for months before feeling the boat rest on dry land. Over the course of a year or more, Noah's family of eight experienced the faithfulness of God's protection, watched what God said would happen really happen, and then saw the sign of God's promise—a rainbow—that meant the earth would never again be destroyed by water.

Every time you see a rainbow, think about Noah's story and praise God for His power and goodness!

The Tower of Babel

Selected Scripture from Genesis 11

The whole earth had one language and one speech. [The people] said, "Come, let us build ourselves a city, and a tower whose top is in the heavens; let us make a name for ourselves, lest we be scattered abroad over the face of the whole earth."

The LORD came down to see the city and the tower which the sons of men had built. The LORD said, "Let Us go down and there confuse their language, that they may not understand one another's speech." So the LORD scattered them abroad from there over the face of all the earth, and they ceased building the city. Therefore its name is called Babel, because there the LORD confused the language of all the earth; and from there the LORD scattered them abroad.

FROM BILLY GRAHAM

The people in Babel thought they didn't need God. They were more concerned with making themselves look great than praising God for being truly great.

The Bible warns, "Pride goes before destruction, and a haughty spirit before a fall" (Proverbs 16:18). Why is pride such a big problem? For one thing, it keeps us from seeing our faults. Pride tells us we are better than we really are, so we feel no need to confess our sins or change our ways.

Pride also hurts our relationships. We can be proud for many reasons: our possessions, physical appearance, abilities, achievements, and so forth. Whatever the reason, however, pride always puts us above others. No one likes an arrogant, prideful person.

Most of all, pride makes us start to think that we don't need God. Once we understand how great God is, we will become more humble. It is hard to be proud when we compare ourselves to God instead of other people.

Father Abraham

God's Instructions, God's Promises

Selected Scripture from Genesis 12, 15, and 17

Now the Lord had said to Abram:

> "Get out of your country,
>   To a land that I will show you.
>   I will make you a great nation;
>   I will bless you,
>   And in you all the families of the earth shall be blessed."

So Abram departed. Abram took Sarai his wife and Lot his brother's son, and all their possessions, and they came to the land of Canaan.

The word of the Lord came to Abram, saying, "Do not be afraid, Abram. I am your shield, your exceedingly great reward."

But Abram said, "Lord GOD, what will You give me, seeing I go childless?"

The word of the LORD came to him, saying, "One who will come from your own body shall be your heir. Look now toward heaven, and count the stars if you are able. So shall your descendants be."

When Abram was ninety-nine years old, the LORD appeared to Abram and said, "I am Almighty God. My covenant is with you, and you shall be a father of many nations. No longer shall your name be Abram, but your name shall be Abraham. I will make you exceedingly fruitful; and I will make nations of you, and kings shall come from you. And I will establish My covenant between Me and you and your descendants after you, for an everlasting covenant, to be God to you and your descendants after you.

"As for Sarai your wife, Sarah shall be her name. And I will give you a son by her; then I will bless her, and she shall be a mother of nations."

Just as God Had Promised

Selected Scripture from Genesis 18 and 21

The LORD appeared to [Abraham] as he was sitting in the tent door in the heat of the day.

And He said, "I will certainly return to you, and behold, Sarah your wife shall have a son."

Sarah was listening in the tent door; and Sarah had passed the age of childbearing. Therefore Sarah laughed within herself.

And the LORD said to Abraham, "Why did Sarah laugh? Is anything too hard for the LORD? Sarah shall have a son."

And the LORD did for Sarah as He had spoken. Sarah conceived and bore Abraham a son. Abraham called his son Isaac. Abraham was one hundred years old when his son Isaac was born.

FROM BILLY GRAHAM

Can you blame Abraham and Sarah for doubting God's promise? Sarah had been childless all their married life, and now she was approaching the age of ninety. Could anything be more impossible? Ninety-year-old women simply do not have children.

But God gently reminded them that nothing is too hard for Him. And the following year the impossible happened: Isaac was born. God's promise to Abraham that he would become the father of a great nation (and the ancestor of Jesus Christ) could now be fulfilled.

Remember Abraham and Sarah the next time you have what seems to be an impossible problem. Nothing was too hard for God then—and nothing is too hard for Him today.

Esau's Stolen Blessing

Selected Scripture from Genesis 25 and 27

Isaac grew up and married Rebekah, and they had twin boys: Esau was Isaac's favorite, and Jacob was Rebekah's favorite. Isaac's blessing and most of his things would go to the older son, Esau, when he died. Jacob was jealous and wanted to steal what was rightfully Esau's.

When Isaac was old and could not see, he called Esau and said, "Go hunt game for me. Make me savory food, that my soul may bless you."

Rebekah overheard this. She prepared savory food and put goatskins on Jacob so that Isaac would think that smooth-skinned Jacob was his hairy brother, Esau.

[Jacob] went to his father and said, "I am Esau. Please eat of my game, that your soul may bless me."

Isaac said, "Please come near, that I may feel you, whether you are really my son Esau." So Jacob went near his father, and [Isaac] did not recognize him, because his hands were hairy like his brother Esau's hands; so [Isaac] blessed [Jacob].

As soon as Isaac finished blessing Jacob, Esau came in. He had made savory food, and brought it to his father, and said, "Let my father arise and eat of his son's game, that your soul may bless me."

Isaac trembled exceedingly. "Your brother came with deceit and has taken your blessing."

So Esau hated Jacob.

FROM BILLY GRAHAM

It was wrong for Rebekah and Jacob to be dishonest and trick Isaac. God has commanded, "You shall not . . . lie to one another" (Leviticus 19:11). *Honesty* means exactly what it says. People should be able to trust our word because we tell the truth (even if it gets us in trouble). They also know we won't use half-truths or deceit to take advantage of them. God's people are honest and trustworthy.

Jacob's Ladder

Selected Scripture from Genesis 28

Esau was so angry with Jacob that he wanted to kill Jacob. So Jacob moved away, and one night during his travels he was sleeping outside.

He dreamed, and behold, a ladder was set up on the earth, and its top reached to heaven; and there the angels of God were ascending and descending on it.

The LORD stood above it and said: "I am the LORD God of Abraham your father and the God of Isaac; the land on which you lie I will give to you and your descendants. Your descendants shall be as the dust of the earth; you shall spread abroad to the west and the east, to the north and the south; and in you and in your [descendants] all the families of the earth shall be blessed. I am with you and will keep you wherever you go, and will bring you back to this land; for I will not leave you until I have done what I have spoken to you."

Jacob awoke from his sleep and said, "How awesome is this place! This is none other than the house of God, and this is the gate of heaven!"

Jacob made a vow, saying, "If God will be with me [and help me], so that I come back to my father's house in peace, then the Lord shall be my God."

FROM BILLY GRAHAM

Just as God promised to be with Jacob, He has promised to be with you in every situation. He has said, "I will never leave you nor forsake you" (Hebrews 13:5). God does not lie, nor does He change His mind. What if He did? Then we wouldn't have any reason to depend on Him; His Word could not be trusted. But He doesn't lie, and He doesn't change His mind—because He is perfect and holy, and He loves us. We can trust His promises!

Joseph: Servant, Leader, Hero

From Favorite Son to Foreign Slave

Selected Scripture from Genesis 37 and 39

[Jacob] loved Joseph more than all his children. He made him a tunic of many colors. When his brothers saw that their father loved him more, they hated him.

The brothers planned to kill Joseph.

They stripped Joseph of his tunic of many colors and cast him into a pit.

Judah said to his brothers, "What profit is there if we kill our brother? Let us sell him to the Ishmaelites." His brothers listened and sold him to the Ishmaelites for twenty shekels of silver. And they took Joseph to Egypt.

The brothers sent Joseph's tunic covered with goat's blood to their father.

He recognized it and said, "It is my son's tunic. A wild beast has devoured him." Then Jacob mourned for his son many days.

Potiphar, an officer of Pharaoh, bought [Joseph] from the Ishmaelites. The LORD was with Joseph, and he was a successful man. His master saw that the LORD was with him and made all he did prosper. So Joseph found favor in [Potiphar's] sight. Then [Potiphar] made him overseer of his house. The LORD blessed the Egyptian's house for Joseph's sake.

After his brothers sold him into slavery, Joseph could have become angry with God. But instead, Joseph turned to Him.

God responded not by removing Joseph from his difficult situation but by helping him right where he was. When Joseph turned to God, He blessed Joseph's work and brought good things to him and those around him. Here we can see a marvelous truth of the Bible: when we reach out to God in faith, He gets involved with us right where we are.

When Joseph was hurt, he still trusted the Lord and followed Him. God heard Joseph's call for help, just as He will hear you if you'll turn to Him.

Pharaoh's Dreams

Selected Scripture from Genesis 39, 41–42

Then Potiphar's wife accused Joseph of something he did not do. Even though Joseph was innocent, Potiphar put him in prison.

But the LORD was with Joseph and showed him mercy, and He gave him favor in the sight of the keeper of the prison.

Pharaoh had a dream and called Joseph. "I have heard that you can understand a dream, to interpret it."

Joseph answered, "It is not in me; God will give Pharaoh an answer. God has shown Pharaoh what He is about to do: Seven years of great plenty will come throughout all of Egypt; but after them seven years of famine will arise, and all the plenty will be forgotten; and the famine will deplete the land."

Then Pharaoh said to Joseph, "Inasmuch as God has shown you all this, you shall be over my house, and all my people shall be ruled according to your word."

In the seven plentiful years the ground brought forth abundantly. So [Joseph] gathered up all the food of the seven years, and laid up the food in the cities.

The seven years of famine began to come, as Joseph had said. The famine was in all lands, but in Egypt there was bread. So all countries came to Joseph in Egypt to buy grain.

Joseph's ten brothers went to buy grain in Egypt and bowed down before him.

Joseph recognized his brothers, but they did not recognize him.

Joseph Forgives

Selected Scripture from Genesis 43, 45, and 50

Joseph's youngest brother, Benjamin, was not among the brothers who went to Egypt. Wanting to see Benjamin, Joseph told his brothers that they could have food if one brother stayed in Egypt while the other brothers took food back to Egypt and then returned with Benjamin. Their father, Jacob, did not like that plan.

Now the famine was severe. When they had eaten up the grain which they had brought from Egypt, their father said, "Go back, buy us a little food. Take your brother also. And may God Almighty give you mercy before the man, that he may release your other brother and Benjamin."

So the men went to Egypt; and they stood before Joseph.

Joseph could not restrain himself: "I am Joseph your brother, whom you sold into Egypt. But do not be grieved or angry with yourselves because you sold me. God sent me before you to save your lives.

"But as for you, you meant evil against me; but God meant it for good, in order to bring it about as it is this day, to save many people alive."

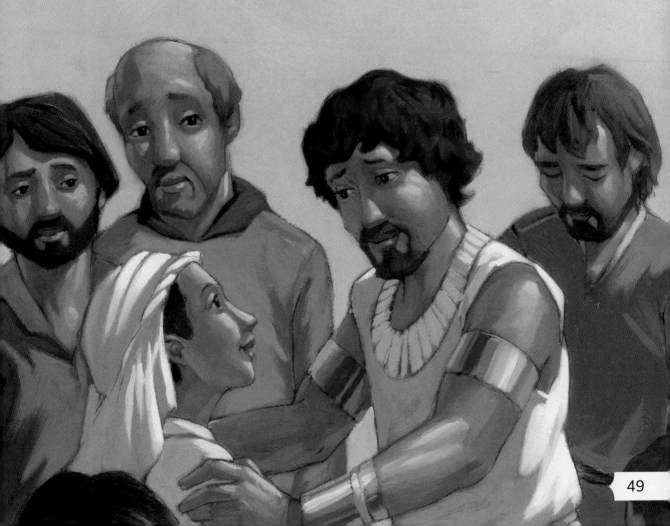

God tells us to forgive people who have wronged us—even if we don't think they deserve it. He calls us to be patient with each other and forgive others as He forgives us (Colossians 3:13). This command is hard to obey, but if we don't, we will just keep on being angry and unhappy. With God's help, we can be like Joseph and deal with this kind of problem in a way that honors Him.

First, we need to be honest about anything we did wrong and ask for God's forgiveness. Then we need to ask the person to forgive us as well—even if they may say no.

Next, we need to ask God to help us forgive the one who hurt us. The only way to do this, I believe, is to realize that God has forgiven us for every wrong thing we have done. We don't deserve His forgiveness, yet He freely offers it to us. Ask Him to replace the hurt and anger in your heart with His love, and He will.

God's Job for Moses

Baby Moses

Selected Scripture from Exodus 1–2

Now there arose a new king over Egypt, who did not know Joseph. And he said to his people, "Look, the people of the children of Israel are more and mightier than we; come, let us deal shrewdly with them, lest they multiply." Therefore they set taskmasters over them to afflict them with their burdens.

Pharaoh then commanded that every newborn son in Israelite homes be killed. Then Moses was born, but his mother protected him by making a floating basket for him.

She hid him three months. But when she could no longer hide him, she took an ark of bulrushes for him, daubed it with asphalt and pitch, put the child in it, and laid it in the reeds by the river's bank. And his sister stood afar off, to know what would be done to him.

Baby Moses floated down the river in the basket, and before long Pharaoh's daughter saw the basket.

She sent her maid to get it. And when she opened it, she saw the child, and behold, the baby wept. So she had compassion on him, and said, "This is one of the Hebrews' children."

Then [Moses'] sister said to Pharaoh's daughter, "Shall I go and call a nurse for you from the Hebrew women, that she may nurse the child for you?"

And Pharaoh's daughter said to her, "Go." So the maiden went and called the child's mother. Then Pharaoh's daughter said to her, "Take this child away and nurse him for me, and I will give you your wages." So the woman took the child and nursed him. And the child grew, and she brought him to Pharaoh's daughter, and he became her son.

The Burning Bush

Selected Scripture from Exodus 3

Moses was tending the flock of his father-in-law. The Angel of the Lord appeared to him in a fire from the midst of a bush. He looked, and behold, the bush was burning with fire, but the bush was not consumed.

God called to him from the midst of the bush and said, "Moses, Moses!"

And he said, "Here I am."

Then He said, "Take your sandals off your feet, for where you stand is holy ground." He said, "I am the God of your father—the God of Abraham, the God of Isaac, and the God of Jacob." And Moses hid his face, for he was afraid to look upon God.

The LORD said: "I have surely seen the oppression of My people, and have heard their cry because of their taskmasters, for I know their sorrows. I will send you to Pharaoh that you may bring My people out of Egypt."

But Moses said to God, "Who am I that I should go to Pharaoh, and that I should bring the children of Israel out of Egypt?"

So He said, "I will certainly be with you."

FROM BILLY GRAHAM

When God called Moses to be part of His important work in Egypt, Moses didn't think he could do what God was asking him to do. Moses was just an ordinary person, and he thought God should use someone more special and gifted.

But the Bible is full of ordinary people. As a matter of fact, God uses ordinary people far more often than He does the rich, powerful, and famous. Jesus chose ordinary people as His disciples.

You might notice how other people are special and gifted, but so are you. You are very valuable to God because He made you just as you are. God makes all of His people able to serve Him. Ask God to show you His plan for your life. When you discover God's plan for your life and act on it, you will begin to see yourself as God already sees you: as an extraordinary person whom God loves and wants to be part of His important work!

Asking to Leave Egypt

Selected Scripture from Exodus 5, 7–12

Moses told Pharaoh, "Thus says the LORD God of Israel: 'Let My people go.'"

Pharaoh said, "Who is the LORD, that I should obey His voice? I do not know the LORD, nor will I let Israel go."

Because Pharaoh was stubborn and refused to let God's people leave Egypt, God said He would show Pharaoh His power by bringing plagues to Egypt.

All the waters in the river turned to blood. The fish in the river died, the river stank, and the Egyptians could not drink the water. Frogs came up and covered the land of Egypt. The dust of the earth became lice on man and beast. Thick swarms of flies came into the house of Pharaoh, into his servants' houses, and into all of Egypt. All the livestock of Egypt died.

Then [came] sores on man and beast. Hail struck the whole land of Egypt, all that was in the field. Locusts went up over all of Egypt. They ate every herb of the land and all the fruit of the trees which the hail had left. [Then] there was thick darkness in all of Egypt three days.

The Lord said to Moses, "I will bring one more plague on Pharaoh and on Egypt. Afterward he will let you go." At midnight the Lord struck all the firstborn in the land of Egypt, from the firstborn of Pharaoh to the firstborn of the captive in the dungeon, and all the firstborn of livestock. There was a great cry in Egypt, for there was not a house where there was not one dead.

[Pharaoh] said, "Rise, go out from among my people. And go, serve the Lord as you have said."

Crossing the Red Sea—on Dry Land!

Selected Scripture from Exodus 14

After God's people left Egypt, the king regretted his decision to let them go and led six hundred chariots in pursuit of Israel. The people were terrified, but Moses said, "Do not be afraid. The LORD will fight for you" (Exodus 14:13–14).

The LORD said to Moses, "Lift up your rod, and stretch out your hand over the sea."

Moses stretched out his hand over the sea; and the LORD caused the sea to go back and made the sea into dry land. So the children of Israel went into the midst of the sea on the dry ground, and the waters were a wall to them on their right hand and on their left. And the Egyptians went after them into the midst of the sea, all Pharaoh's horses, his chariots, and his horsemen.

Then Moses stretched out his rod again, and the sea washed over the Egyptian army, killing every soldier.

So the LORD saved Israel that day out of the hand of the Egyptians.

FROM BILLY GRAHAM

God didn't want the Egyptians to capture the Israelites. He did something that seemed impossible—changing a sea to dry land—to accomplish His purpose. One of the biggest blessings my mother gave me was teaching me at the age of ten that "God is a Spirit, infinite, eternal, and unchangeable in His being, wisdom, power, holiness, justice, goodness, and truth." That definition of God has been with me all my life. There is no limit to God. There is no limit to His wisdom. There is no limit to His power. There is no limit to His love. When we know this in our hearts, it helps us remember that He is able to accomplish things that we can't do ourselves!

The Ten Commandments

Selected Scripture from Exodus 19–31

Before God led the Israelites into the Promised Land, He wanted them to understand and follow His commands. So Moses met with God at the top of a mountain for forty days and nights, and when he came down, he carried two stone tablets. God had written these Ten Commandments on them:

"You shall have no other gods before Me.

"You shall not bow down to [other gods] nor serve them.

"You shall not take the name of the LORD your God in vain.

"Remember the Sabbath day, to keep it holy. Six days you shall labor and do all your work, but the seventh day is the Sabbath of the LORD your God. In it you shall do no work.

"Honor your father and your mother.

"You shall not murder.

"You shall not commit adultery.

"You shall not steal.

"You shall not bear false witness against your neighbor.

"You shall not covet anything that is your neighbor's."

FROM BILLY GRAHAM

The Ten Commandments help us understand what is right and what is wrong. The first four commandments show that our main priority is to love God; the other six guide our love of other people.

God has given us these standards for another reason: He loves us, and He wants what is best for us. What happens when people don't do these things? What happens when people lie and steal and do other evil things all the time? People hurt other people, and they sin against God.

Thank God that He cares about us so much that He has told us how to live, and ask Him to help you follow Him in everything you do.

The Spies and Rahab of Jericho

Rahab's Help

Selected Scripture from Joshua 1–2

After Moses died, God commanded Joshua to lead the people into the Promised Land, saying, "Be strong and of good courage; do not be afraid, nor be dismayed, for the LORD your God is with you wherever you go" (Joshua 1:9). Joshua sent spies to the land to see what it was like, and the spies stayed at Rahab's house.

So the king of Jericho sent [messengers] to Rahab, saying, "Bring out the [spies] who have entered your house."

She said, "Yes, the [spies] came to me, but I did not know where they were from. When it was dark, the [spies] went out. Where the [spies] went I do not know; pursue them quickly, for you may overtake them." (But she had brought them up to the roof and hidden them with the stalks of flax, which she had laid in order on the roof.) Then the [king's messengers] pursued [the spies].

Rahab went up on her roof and asked the spies to save her family when Israel attacked Jericho because Rahab had just saved them. The spies agreed.

Then she let them down by a rope through the window, for her house was on the city wall. And she said, "Get to the mountain. Hide there three days."

So the [spies] said to her: "Bind this line of scarlet cord in the window, and bring all your father's household to your own home."

Jericho's Crumbling Walls

Selected Scripture from Joshua 6

God had a strange plan for Joshua. The Lord told the army to march around the city of Jericho once a day for six days and then, on the seventh day, to march around Jericho seven times. Then, God explained, the priests would blow their trumpets, the people would shout, and the wall would fall down.

And [Joshua] said to the people, "March around the city." So it was. Then they came into the camp and lodged. So they did six days.

On the seventh day they rose early and marched around the city seven times. And the seventh time, when the priests blew the trumpets, Joshua said to the people: "Shout, for the LORD has given you the city!"

So the people shouted. The wall fell down flat. Then the people [of Israel] took the city.

Joshua spared Rahab the harlot, her father's household, and all that she had, because she hid the messengers whom Joshua sent to spy out Jericho.

God's battle plan must have seemed crazy to Joshua. When had marching, blowing trumpets, and shouting ever defeated a whole city? But Joshua didn't question God. He was loyal, obedient, and courageous.

Joshua stood before Jericho. Jericho was a great fortress. As Joshua was praying, he knew God was with him and was humbled before Him. No wonder God gave him great victory!

Matthew 17:20 says, "If you have faith as a mustard seed, you will say to this mountain, 'Move from here to there,' and it will move." Joshua put his faith in God's power and plan, and big things happened! When God's commands don't make sense, remember that God knows what He is doing. You can trust Him to do what is right according to His perfect plan.

God Guides Through Deborah

Selected Scripture from Judges 4

When Israel disobeyed God and stopped worshiping Him, He let the king of Canaan rule over them for twenty years. The Canaanites were cruel to the Israelites. God said He would free them, but they would have to obey Him. Deborah, the wise judge over the Israelites, trusted God and shared God's message with people. She wanted to help Barak, the Israelite army commander, trust God and defeat Sisera, the Canaanite army commander.

[Deborah] called for Barak and said, "Has not the LORD God of Israel commanded, 'Go and deploy troops at Mount Tabor; take with you ten thousand men; and against you I will deploy Sisera with his chariots and his multitude; and I will deliver him into your hand'?"

Barak said to her, "If you will go with me, then I will go; but if you will not go with me, I will not go!"

So she said, "I will surely go with you." Then Deborah arose.

Sisera gathered all his nine hundred chariots of iron, and all the people who were with him.

Then Deborah said to Barak, "Up! For this is the day in which the LORD has delivered Sisera into your hand. Has not the LORD gone out before you?"

And God gave them great victory over the enemy, just as He promised.

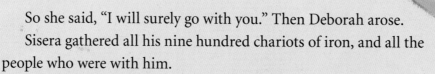

Deborah trusted God right away, but Barak needed some encouragement. It's hard to trust God when we're in a scary situation or when everything seems to be going wrong. Fear comes much easier to us than faith. But never forget: *fear can overcome faith, but faith can also overcome fear.* Faith isn't pretending our problems don't exist, nor is it simply wishful thinking. Faith points us beyond our problems to the hope we have in Christ. True faith involves *trust*—trust in what Christ has done for us, and trust in God's goodness and mercy.

Once we realize God is in control and He holds us in His loving hands, we can be braver about doing hard things. Just like the psalmist said, we do not have to be afraid because the Lord is with us (Psalm 118:6).

Gideon's Big Victory

Selected Scripture from Judges 6–8

The angel of the Lord appeared to Gideon and called him to lead Israel against the Midianites. God promised to be with Gideon and to give Israel victory over Midian. Gideon's army had thirty-two thousand men. But God told Gideon to reduce the size of his army to only three hundred men—a very small number compared to the Midian army. God wanted His people to see that they would win not because of their own strength but because He was with them.

The Lord said to Gideon, "By three hundred men I will save you and deliver the Midianites into your hand. Let all the other people go."

On the same night the Lord said to him, "Arise, go down against the camp, for I have delivered it into your hand."

[Gideon] divided the three hundred men into three companies, and he put a trumpet into every man's hand, with empty pitchers, and torches inside the pitchers. And he said, "When I blow the trumpet, then you also blow the trumpets, and say, 'The sword of the Lord and of Gideon!'"

So Gideon and the hundred men with him came to the camp. Then the three companies blew the trumpets and broke the pitchers and they cried, "The sword of the Lord and of Gideon!" When the three hundred blew the trumpets, the Lord set every [Midianite] sword against his companion throughout the whole camp.

Thus Midian was subdued before the children of Israel. And the country was quiet for forty years.

It is true that God's strength is made perfect in weakness. Otherwise, it would not be God's strength, nor would He get the glory. That is why throughout the Old Testament God ordered the leaders of Israel to reduce the size of their armies. God wanted the faith of man to be placed in Him and not in physical strength.

Do you need God's strength for something you are facing? You can have it. Just ask!

Strong Samson

Selected Scripture from Judges 14–16

Samson was an Israelite leader who could overpower everyone, even wild animals. He did not, however, honor God with his abilities. The Philistines couldn't defeat him until Delilah, the woman Samson loved, agreed to help them capture Samson by finding out the secret of his strength. He had taken a solemn vow to serve God, and as an outward sign of that vow, he was forbidden to cut his hair.

[Delilah] pestered [Samson] daily with her words and pressed him, so that his soul was vexed to death, that he told her all his heart, and said to her, "No razor has ever come upon my head, for I have been a Nazirite to God from my mother's womb. If I am shaven, then my strength will leave me, and I shall become weak, and be like any other man."

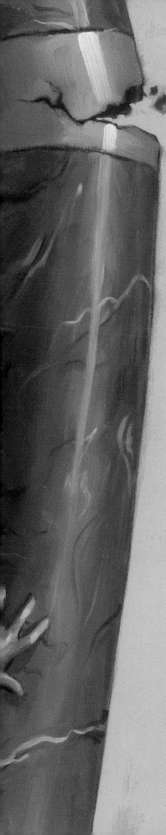

Delilah had someone shave Samson's head while he was asleep, and he lost his strength. Then the Philistines captured him, blinded him, and put him in prison. But his hair kept growing.

Then Samson called to the LORD, saying, "O Lord GOD, remember me, I pray! Strengthen me, I pray, just this once, O God, that I may with one blow take vengeance on the Philistines for my two eyes!" And Samson took hold of the two middle pillars which supported the temple, and he braced himself against them, one on his right and the other on his left. Then Samson said, "Let me die with the Philistines!" And he pushed with all his might, and the temple fell on the lords and all the people who were in it.

FROM BILLY GRAHAM

The Bible tells us that Samson was strong. Samson was handsome. God blessed him in many ways.

But as a young man, Samson made many wrong choices and did many wrong things. By the end of his life, he was sorry he hadn't followed God. The Bible says, "Humble yourselves under the mighty hand of God" (1 Peter 5:6)—and that's what Samson finally did. Ask God to help you make right choices in life—choices that are in line with His will.

Ruth, the Loyal Daughter-in-Law

Staying with Naomi

Selected Scripture from Ruth 1

Now it came to pass, there was a famine in the land. And a certain man of Bethlehem went to dwell in the country of Moab, he and his wife [Naomi] and his two sons. Naomi's husband died; and she was left, and her two sons. Now they took wives of the women of Moab: Orpah and Ruth. They dwelt there about ten years. Then both [sons] died.

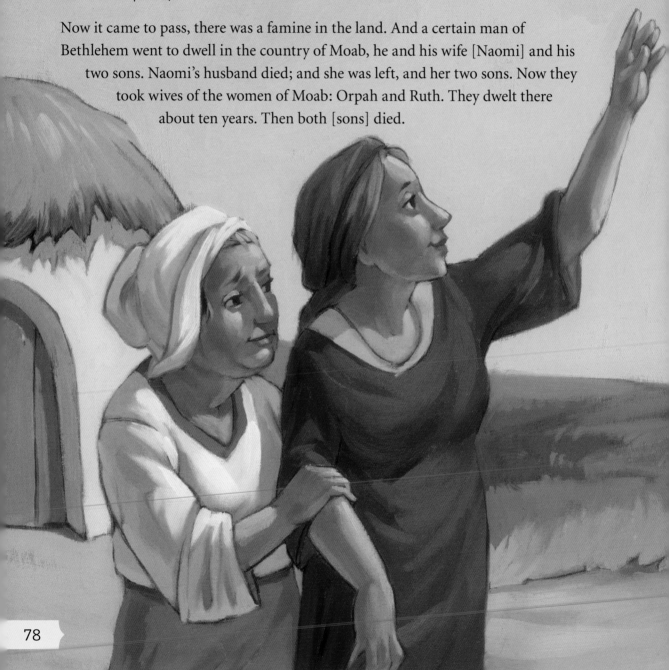

Therefore [Naomi] and her two daughters-in-law went on the way to return to Judah. Naomi said to her two daughters-in-law, "Go, return each to her mother's house. The LORD grant that you may find rest, each in the house of her husband."

Orpah kissed her mother-in-law, but Ruth clung to her. Ruth said:

"Wherever you go, I will go;
Your people shall be my people,
And your God, my God."

The two of them went to Bethlehem.

Boaz, Ruth, and Baby Obed

Selected Scripture from Ruth 2 and 4

A wealthy man named Boaz, who was a relative of Naomi's husband, lived in Bethlehem. Ruth was gleaning—picking up grain harvesters had left behind—in a field that Boaz owned.

Boaz said to Ruth, "My daughter, do not go to glean in another field. When you are thirsty, drink from what the young men have drawn."

She bowed and said, "Why have I found favor in your eyes?"

Boaz said, "It has been fully reported to me, all that you have done for your mother-in-law. A full reward be given you by the LORD God of Israel."

Boaz commanded his young men, saying, "Let grain from the bundles fall purposely for her; leave it that she may glean, and do not rebuke her."

Boaz took Ruth and she became his wife; and she bore a son. They called his name Obed. He is the father of Jesse, the father of David.

FROM BILLY GRAHAM

The Bible teaches us to honor our parents (Exodus 20:12). When we are children, we do that by obeying them. Even when we grow up, it's still important to love, respect, and honor our parents. And we honor them by helping them in whatever way we can.

Ruth's mother-in-law, Naomi, needed help because Naomi's husband and her sons had died, and she wanted to go back home to Israel. So Ruth decided to help Naomi and go back to Israel with her. What can you do to help your mom or dad today?

The Desire of Hannah's Heart

Selected Scripture from 1 Samuel 1–2

A man named Elkanah had two wives: Peninnah had children; Hannah didn't. Every year Elkanah and his wives went to Shiloh to worship God.

[One year] Hannah arose after they had finished eating and drinking in Shiloh. Now Eli the priest was sitting by the doorpost of the tabernacle. And she prayed to the Lord and wept in anguish. Then she made a vow and said, "O Lord of hosts, if You give [me] a male child, then I will give him to the Lord all the days of his life."

As she continued praying, Eli watched her mouth. Eli said to her, "Go in peace, and the God of Israel grant your petition which you have asked of Him."

The Lord remembered her. Hannah conceived and bore a son, and called his name Samuel.

Now when [Hannah] had weaned [Samuel], she took him to the house of the LORD in Shiloh. And she said [to Eli the priest], "For this child I prayed, and the LORD has granted me my petition. Therefore as long as he lives he shall be lent to the LORD."

FROM BILLY GRAHAM

How do you respond to troubles? Hannah shows us what we should do: before anything else, turn to God in prayer (James 5:13, 16). Prayer helps us remember we can't solve everything on our own.

Prayer is a way for us to show that we believe in God's power and love. We aren't trying to trick God into doing what we want—we are looking to Him to bless us and help us according to His perfect plan for us. When troubles come, may prayer be the first thing you do.

Samuel's "Here I Am, God!"

Selected Scripture from 1 Samuel 2–3

The child Samuel grew in stature, and in favor both with the Lord and men.

[One night] the Lord called Samuel. And he answered, "Here I am!" He ran to Eli and said, "Here I am, for you called me."

[Eli] said, "I did not call; lie down again." And [Samuel] went and lay down.

The Lord called yet again, "Samuel!"

Samuel arose and went to Eli, and said, "Here I am, for you called me." He answered, "I did not call, my son; lie down again."

The Lord called Samuel the third time. So he arose and went to Eli, and said, "Here I am, for you did call me."

Then Eli perceived that the Lord had called the boy. Therefore Eli said to Samuel, "Go, lie down; if He calls you, say, 'Speak, Lord, for Your servant hears.'" So Samuel went and lay down.

Now the Lord came and called, "Samuel! Samuel!"

And Samuel answered, "Speak, for Your servant hears."

So Samuel grew, and the Lord was with him. All Israel knew that Samuel had been established as a prophet of the Lord.

God can use anyone who sincerely says, "Here I am!" just like Samuel did. God can use you to help other people know Jesus.

Jesus said that God's people are the light of the world, and that when we do good things, others will see God's goodness and want to praise Him (Matthew 5:14, 16). Do others see something different about you? Are you kind and thoughtful? Do you share or let other people go first? Do you help people and encourage them?

All around you are people who do not know God, and you might be surprised to find that some of them wonder about God. Pray that God will give you the right words to say when He opens the door. Even a few words of encouragement or concern can be used of God. Be like Samuel, ready to say, "Here I am!" when God calls you to tell others about Him.

Brave and Loving David

David and the Giant

Selected Scripture from 1 Samuel 17

The Philistines gathered their armies to battle. The Philistines stood on a mountain on one side, and Israel stood on a mountain on the other side, with a valley between them.

A champion went out from the Philistines, named Goliath, whose height was six cubits and a span [more than nine feet]. He cried out to Israel, "Choose a man, and let him come down to me. If he is able to kill me, we will be your servants. But if I kill him, then you shall serve us." Saul and all Israel were greatly afraid.

Jesse had eight sons, and the three oldest had gone with King Saul to fight the battle. Jesse sent his youngest son, David, to check on his brothers. When David came to the army camp, he heard Goliath saying bad things about God and challenging the Israelite soldiers to fight.

Then David said to Saul, "Your servant will go and fight this Philistine."

David the shepherd had killed both lion and bear to protect his sheep. He knew the God who delivered him from the lion and bear would protect him from Goliath.

[David] took his staff; and he chose for himself five smooth stones from the brook, and put them in a shepherd's bag, and his sling was in his hand. And he drew near to the Philistine.

Then David said to the Philistine, "You come to me with a sword, with a spear, and with a javelin. But I come to you in the name of the LORD of hosts, whom you have defied. The battle is the LORD's, and He will give you into our hands."

David took out a stone; and he slung it and struck the Philistine in his forehead, and he fell on his face to the earth. So David prevailed over the Philistine with a sling and a stone, and struck the Philistine and killed him. When the Philistines saw that their champion was dead, they fled.

Young David faced a giant named Goliath, a member of the Philistine nation—a bitter enemy of God's people. Goliath was more than nine feet tall and clothed with heavy armor. His spear was about the size of a tree trunk. Goliath was one of the largest men in recorded history, and David volunteered to fight Goliath for God's army.

Goliath had David out-armed and out-experienced. Goliath was a great warrior; David was not. His only weapon was a slingshot—and a deep dependence on God. And God gave him victory.

David and Jonathan's Friendship

Selected Scripture from 1 Samuel 18–20

After David defeated Goliath, David met King Saul and Saul's son, Jonathan.

The soul of Jonathan was knit to the soul of David, and Jonathan loved him as his own soul. Jonathan and David made a covenant, because he loved him as his own soul. And Jonathan took off the robe that was on him and gave it to David, with his armor, even to his sword and his bow and his belt.

Unfortunately, King Saul grew jealous of David's popularity.

Saul spoke to Jonathan his son and to all his servants, that they should kill David; but Jonathan delighted greatly in David. So Jonathan told David, saying, "My father Saul seeks to kill you."

Jonathan was in line to become king. He protected David, even though that meant giving up becoming king himself. He knew that God wanted David to be king, and he was a faithful friend.

Jonathan spoke well of David to Saul his father, and said to him, "Let not the king sin against his servant, against David, because he has not sinned against you, and because his works have been very good toward you. Why then will you sin against innocent blood, to kill David without a cause?"

Ultimately, King Saul still wanted to kill David, and David and Jonathan had to have a tearful good-bye.

Jonathan said to David, "Go in peace, since we have both sworn in the name of the Lord, saying, 'May the Lord be between you and me, and between your descendants and my descendants, forever.'"

FROM BILLY GRAHAM

Jonathan and David were buddies. They stuck together through thick and thin, through hard times and good times. The Bible teaches us to be more concerned about the needs and feelings of others than our own. A true servant of God is someone who encourages others and helps them succeed.

Learn to be a friend to others. A good way to start is to do something practical for someone else who has a need.

David and the Psalms

Selected Scripture from Psalms 23, 139, 145, and 147

Sing praises on the harp to our God,
Who covers the heavens with clouds,
Who prepares rain for the earth,
Who makes grass to grow on the mountains.

You formed my inward parts;
I will praise You, for I am fearfully and wonderfully made.

The LORD is my shepherd;
I shall not want.
He makes me to lie down in green pastures;
He leads me beside the still waters.

Every day I will bless You,
And I will praise Your name forever and ever.
Great is the LORD, and greatly to be praised.

David worshiped God by singing and praying to God. How do you worship God? What is worship anyway?

We worship God when we put our full attention on Him—on His glory, His power, His love, His goodness. That's actually hard to do because, even in church or in our quiet times at home, we get distracted and fail to see God as He truly is.

Notice in these verses why David worshiped God. First, David saw Him as Lord—the all-powerful God of the universe. He recognized, too, that God had made him; he wasn't here by accident but by God's perfect plan. Finally, he worshiped God because God had made him part of His flock, constantly watching over him and providing for his every need.

When we spend time every day praising God for who He is and thanking Him for His love, we are getting a peek at what we will do in heaven. Someday, we will meet this King of the universe, and in His presence we will bow in worship and say, "You are worthy, O Lord, to receive glory and honor and power" (Revelation 4:11)!

The Wise King Solomon

Selected Scripture from 1 Kings 2–3

Before he died, King David told his son Solomon to obey all the commands of the Lord in order to know the Lord's blessing.

God said [to Solomon], "Ask! What shall I give you?"

Solomon said: "You have made Your servant king, but I am a little child. Therefore give to Your servant an understanding heart to judge Your people, that I may discern between good and evil."

The speech pleased the Lord. Then God said: "Because you have asked

this thing, and have not asked long life for yourself, nor have asked riches for yourself, nor have asked the life of your enemies, but have asked for yourself understanding to discern justice, I have given you a wise and understanding heart, so that there has not been anyone like you before you, nor shall any like you arise after you. And I have also given you what you have not asked: both riches and honor, so that there shall not be anyone like you among the kings all your days. So if you walk in My ways, to keep My statutes and My commandments, I will lengthen your days."

Solomon understood that God mattered most of all, and he was wise and faithful. But after a while, he turned away from God. Solomon focused on the things of the world and lived foolishly instead of obeying God, and he became sad.

Wealth, fame, pleasure, power, fancy houses, a reputation for wisdom—you name it, King Solomon achieved it. And yet after gaining everything he had ever wanted, he later concluded that his life was empty and without meaning because he stopped putting God first. His search for lasting happiness had failed.

Don't be deceived; the things of this world will never make you happy. The reason is that you were made to know God— He is more important than anything!

Elijah and the Fire from God

Selected Scripture from 1 Kings 18

The prophet Elijah challenged the prophets of Baal to a showdown: the God who sent fire in answer to prayer would prove He was God. All day long, the prophets of Baal called for their god, and nothing happened. Then Elijah built an altar to God . . .

Elijah took twelve stones. With the stones he built an altar in the name of the LORD; and he made a trench around the altar. He put the wood in order, cut the bull in pieces, and laid it on the wood, and said, "Fill four waterpots with water, and pour it on the burnt sacrifice and on the wood." Then he said, "Do it a second time," and they did it a second time; and he said, "Do it a third time," and they did it a third time. So the water ran all around the altar; and he also filled the trench with water.

Elijah said, "LORD God, let it be known this day that You are God."

Then the fire of the LORD fell and consumed the burnt sacrifice, and the wood and the stones and the dust, and it licked up the water that was in the trench. When all the people saw it, they fell on their faces; and they said, "The LORD, He is God!"

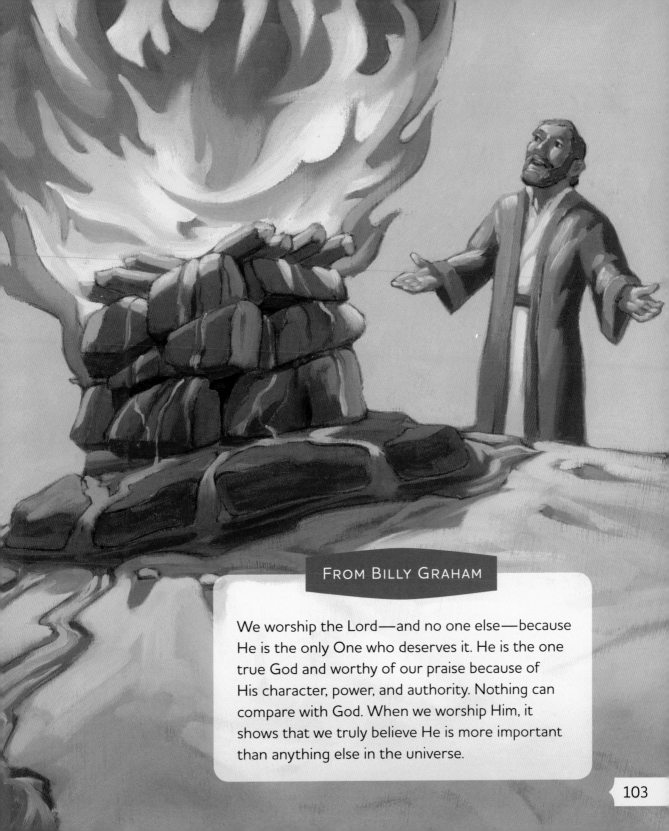

We worship the Lord—and no one else—because He is the only One who deserves it. He is the one true God and worthy of our praise because of His character, power, and authority. Nothing can compare with God. When we worship Him, it shows that we truly believe He is more important than anything else in the universe.

Jonah and the Whale

Selected Scripture from Jonah 1–3

God told Jonah to go to Nineveh to tell the people to stop doing evil, but Jonah did not want to do it. Instead, he went the opposite direction and then got on a boat to try to get farther away. He wound up getting thrown out of the boat and into the sea.

Now the LORD had prepared a great fish to swallow Jonah. And Jonah was in the belly of the fish three days and three nights.

Jonah prayed to the LORD his God from the fish's belly.

So the LORD spoke to the fish, and it vomited Jonah onto dry land.

This time when God told him to go to Nineveh, Jonah went and warned them God would destroy the city in forty days.

The people of Nineveh believed God.

God saw that they turned from their evil way; and God relented from the disaster that He had said He would bring upon them, and He did not do it.

Have you ever been in a car when someone took a wrong turn and ended up going in the wrong direction? The driver probably had to turn around and start going in the opposite direction.

Life is a lot like that. When we realize we are not making God happy with the way we are living, we need to turn around and start going in the opposite direction. We need to start obeying God.

Jonah was going in the wrong direction. Only after he was swallowed by a big fish and lived in its belly for three days did he decide he would turn around and go the right direction. This is called repentance. Repenting when you have done something wrong is an important part of following God.

Isaiah Speaks of a Savior

Selected Scripture from Isaiah 7, 9, and 53

God called Isaiah to be a prophet—to help people hear messages from God and live in ways that honored Him. God told Isaiah that He had a plan to send a Savior for His people, His own Son.

"The Lord Himself will give you a sign: Behold, the virgin shall conceive and bear a Son, and shall call His name Immanuel."

For unto us a Child is born,
Unto us a Son is given;
And the government will be upon His shoulder.
And His name will be called
Wonderful, Counselor, Mighty God,
Everlasting Father, Prince of Peace.
Of the increase of His government and peace
There will be no end,
From that time forward, even forever.

He was wounded for our transgressions,
He was bruised for our iniquities;
And by His stripes we are healed.
Because He poured out His soul unto death,
And He bore the sin of many.

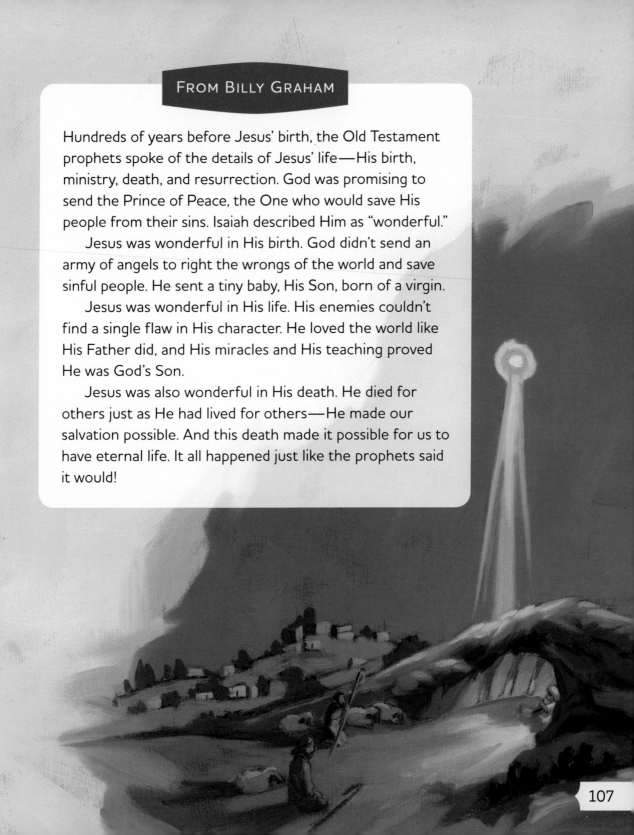

Hundreds of years before Jesus' birth, the Old Testament prophets spoke of the details of Jesus' life—His birth, ministry, death, and resurrection. God was promising to send the Prince of Peace, the One who would save His people from their sins. Isaiah described Him as "wonderful."

Jesus was wonderful in His birth. God didn't send an army of angels to right the wrongs of the world and save sinful people. He sent a tiny baby, His Son, born of a virgin.

Jesus was wonderful in His life. His enemies couldn't find a single flaw in His character. He loved the world like His Father did, and His miracles and His teaching proved He was God's Son.

Jesus was also wonderful in His death. He died for others just as He had lived for others—He made our salvation possible. And this death made it possible for us to have eternal life. It all happened just like the prophets said it would!

Josiah, the Boy King

Selected Scripture from 2 Kings 22–23

Josiah was eight years old when he became king [of Judah]. And he did what was right in the sight of the Lord, and walked in all the ways of his father David.

In the eighteenth year of his reign, Josiah heard God's law, recognized his people's disobedience, and knew God was angry. Josiah called together the elders of Judah and Jerusalem. They went to the house of the Lord and listened as God's Law was read.

Then the king made a covenant before the Lord, to follow the Lord and to keep His commandments and His testimonies and His statutes, with all his heart and all his soul, to perform the words of this covenant that were written in this book. And all the people took a stand for the covenant.

Then the king commanded all the people, saying, "Keep the Passover to the Lord your God, as it is written in this Book of the Covenant." Now before [Josiah] there was no king like him, who turned to the Lord with all his heart, with all his soul, and with all his might, according to all the Law of Moses; nor after him did any arise like him.

Josiah knew that there is only one true compass to guide us in life: the Word of God. In the midst of a thousand different voices calling us to follow them, only one Voice will tell us the truth. The psalmist said, "Your word is a lamp to my feet and a light to my path" (Psalm 119:105). Through the Bible God tells us what is right and how we are to live. He tells us how He loves us and how we can love Him back.

The Bible is our one sure guide in an unsure world. Is it your guide?

Daniel in the Lions' Den

Selected Scripture from Daniel 5–6

Because of their disobedience, God allowed His people to be taken captive by a powerful foreign nation. When Darius became its king, he selected skilled men to be leaders of this nation. And although Daniel was a Jew, he was chosen as one of these. Daniel proved to be such a good leader that the king planned to put him in charge of the whole kingdom. However, the other leaders were jealous of Daniel, so they got King Darius to make a law that said no one could pray to anyone but the king for thirty days. Those who broke that law would be thrown into the lions' den.

When Daniel knew that the [law] was signed, he went home. And in his upper room, with his windows open toward Jerusalem, he knelt down on his knees three times that day, and prayed and gave thanks before his God, as was his custom.

Then these men found Daniel praying. They went before the king: "Have you not signed a decree that every man who petitions any god within thirty days, except you, shall be cast into the den of lions?"

The king said, "The thing is true."

So they said, "Daniel does not show due regard for you, O king, but makes his petition three times a day."

So the king gave the command, and they brought Daniel and cast him into the den of lions. But the king spoke to Daniel, "Your God will deliver you." Then a stone was laid on the mouth of the den.

The king went to his palace and spent the night fasting. Then the king arose very early in the morning and went in haste to the den of lions.

When he came to the den, he cried out to Daniel, "Daniel, has your God been able to deliver you from the lions?"

Then Daniel said to the king, "My God sent His angel and shut the lions' mouths, so that they have not hurt me."

Now the king was exceedingly glad, and commanded that they should take Daniel up out of the den. The king gave the command, and they brought those men who had accused Daniel, and they cast them into the den of lions.

Then King Darius wrote:

I make a decree that in every dominion of my kingdom men must tremble and fear before the God of Daniel.

For He is the living God.

FROM BILLY GRAHAM

The Bible says, "Pray without ceasing" (1 Thessalonians 5:17). When Daniel's life was in danger because he refused to stop worshiping God, he went home and continued to pray just like he always had (Daniel 6:10).

We must learn to pray at all times and in all situations. Nothing can replace a daily time spent alone with God in prayer. But we also can pray throughout the day—sitting in a car, doing chores, going to school.

Walk with God as Daniel did. Pray and trust God no matter what. When Daniel found himself in the lions' den, God was beside him and delivered him.

Esther's Special Job

Selected Scripture from Esther 2–4, 7–8

Esther was a Jew who had been raised by her older cousin Mordecai. Esther was beautiful inside and out. When King Ahasuerus, the ruler of Persia, was looking for a queen, he chose her.

When the turn came for Esther to go in to the king, the king loved Esther more than all the other women; so he set the royal crown upon her head and made her queen.

Haman [one of the king's advisors] said to King Ahasuerus, "There is a certain people [the Jews] scattered and dispersed among the people in all of your kingdom; their laws are different from all other people's, and they do not keep the king's laws. Let a decree be written that they be destroyed." And a decree was written.

When Mordecai learned all that had happened, he cried out with a loud and bitter cry. And in every province where the king's decree arrived, there was great mourning among the Jews.

So Esther's maids and eunuchs told her [about Mordecai], and the queen was deeply distressed.

And Mordecai told Esther: "Do not think in your heart that you will escape in the king's palace any more than all the other Jews. Yet who knows whether you have come to the kingdom for such a time as this?"

Then Esther told Mordecai: "I will go to the king."

It was very dangerous for Esther to meet with the king—because she had not been invited to see him, she could have been killed. But she was brave. She prepared a fancy feast and invited the king and Haman to join her.

The king and Haman went to dine with Queen Esther. And the king said to Esther, "What is your petition, Queen Esther? It shall be granted you."

Queen Esther answered and said, "We have been sold, my people and I, to be destroyed, to be killed."

King Ahasuerus answered and said to Queen Esther, "Who is he, and where is he, who would dare presume in his heart to do such a thing?"

Esther said, "The adversary and enemy is this wicked Haman!"

The king was so angry that he had evil Haman killed. He also made a new decree that allowed the Jews to protect themselves.

In every province and city, wherever the king's command and decree came, the Jews had joy and gladness, a feast and a holiday.

How many of us have the courage of Esther? We so often do only what is easy or popular. Even if, deep inside, we know what the right thing to do is, we hold back because we are afraid of what may happen as a result. If it looks like things will go easily for us, we will take a stand, but if there is any risk involved in standing up for what we know to be right, we will play it safe.

How different from brave Esther! Remember: "God has not given us a spirit of fear, but of power and of love and of a sound mind" (2 Timothy 1:7). Though you may never face what Esther did, don't take the road of a coward; don't give in to fear.

The New Testament

Surprising News for Zacharias

Selected Scripture from Luke 1

A priest named Zacharias and his wife, Elizabeth, loved and obeyed God. They were old and had no children. One day the Lord sent the angel Gabriel to the temple to give Zacharias a surprising message.

The angel said, "Do not be afraid, Zacharias, for your prayer is heard; and your wife Elizabeth will bear you a son, and you shall call his name John. He will be great in the sight of the Lord. And he will turn many of the children of Israel to the Lord their God, to make ready a people prepared for the Lord."

Zacharias asked how he would know this. Gabriel told him he would not be able to speak until the promise happened because he did not believe what he was told.

The people waited for Zacharias, and when he came out, he could not speak; and they perceived that he had seen a vision in the temple.

Elizabeth's full time came for her to be delivered, and she brought forth a son. When her neighbors and relatives heard how the Lord had shown great mercy to her, they rejoiced with her.

After the baby was born, Zacharias wrote that the baby's name would be John. Immediately, he could speak again!

FROM BILLY GRAHAM

When Zacharias heard the words of the angel, he had no physical proof that his wife would have a baby. And it sounded impossible! But God still wanted Zacharias to believe that His word, sent through the angel, was true. Zacharias would have to trust God and have faith to believe in what he couldn't see.

In the same way, we have God's Word before us, full of His promises. Will we respond like Zacharias, or will we believe what God says, even when we do not see any proof?

The Angel's Message for Mary

Selected Scripture from Luke 1

God sent the angel Gabriel to a young woman named Mary.

The angel said to her, "Rejoice, highly favored one, the Lord is with you; blessed are you among women!"

Then the angel said to her, "Do not be afraid, Mary, for you have found favor with God. You will bring forth a Son and shall call His name JESUS. He will be great, and will be called the Son of the Highest."

Then Mary said to the angel, "How can this be, since I do not know a man?"

And the angel answered and said to her, "The Holy Spirit will come upon you, and the power of the Highest will overshadow you; that Holy One who is to be born will be called the Son of God."

Then Mary said, "Behold the maidservant of the Lord! Let it be to me according to your word."

Mary was a teenager when the angel Gabriel appeared before her with this astounding announcement. But by faith Mary told Gabriel that she was the Lord's servant and that she wanted to obey Him (Luke 1:38).

Mary accepted God's will for her life, no matter what it might cost her. Following her example, I pray that God would give me grace and courage to be faithful to Him, no matter what price I may be called on to pay. My hope is that you will pray that prayer too.

Baby Jesus Is Born!

Selected Scripture from Luke 2

And it came to pass in those days that a decree went out from Caesar Augustus that all the world should be registered. So all went to be registered, everyone to his own city.

Joseph also went up from Galilee, out of the city of Nazareth, into Judea, to the city of David, which is called Bethlehem, because he was of the house and lineage of David, to be registered with Mary, his betrothed wife, who was with child. So it was, that while they were there, the days were completed for her to be delivered. And she brought forth her firstborn Son, and wrapped Him in swaddling cloths, and laid Him in a manger, because there was no room for them in the inn.

FROM BILLY GRAHAM

It would have made sense to expect God to tear open the heavens and come down to earth in majesty and power on that first Christmas night—but He didn't.

Instead, on that quiet night in Bethlehem, a virgin mother laid her squalling newborn baby into a manger designed to feed cattle. The lowing cows, the sweet-smelling hay, and the dark sky lit by a magnificent star provided the setting.

Humble shepherds joined the carpenter-husband to witness the miracle and praise God for what He was doing. The birth of Jesus Christ—the Son of God, our Savior—went unnoticed by the vast majority of the world that first Christmas night, but no event in human history was more significant. May His birth—and all it means—not go unnoticed in our lives!

A Surprise for Some Shepherds

Selected Scripture from Luke 2

Now there were in the same country shepherds living out in the fields, keeping watch over their flock by night. And behold, an angel of the Lord stood before them, and the glory of the Lord shone around them, and they were greatly afraid. Then the angel said to them, "Do not be afraid, for I bring you good tidings of great joy which will be to all people. For there is born to you this day in the city of David a Savior, who is Christ the Lord. And this will be the sign to you: You will find a Babe wrapped in swaddling cloths, lying in a manger."

And suddenly there was with the angel a multitude of the heavenly host praising God.

And [the shepherds] came with haste and found Mary and Joseph, and the Babe lying in a manger. Then the shepherds returned, glorifying and praising God for all the things that they had heard and seen, as it was told them.

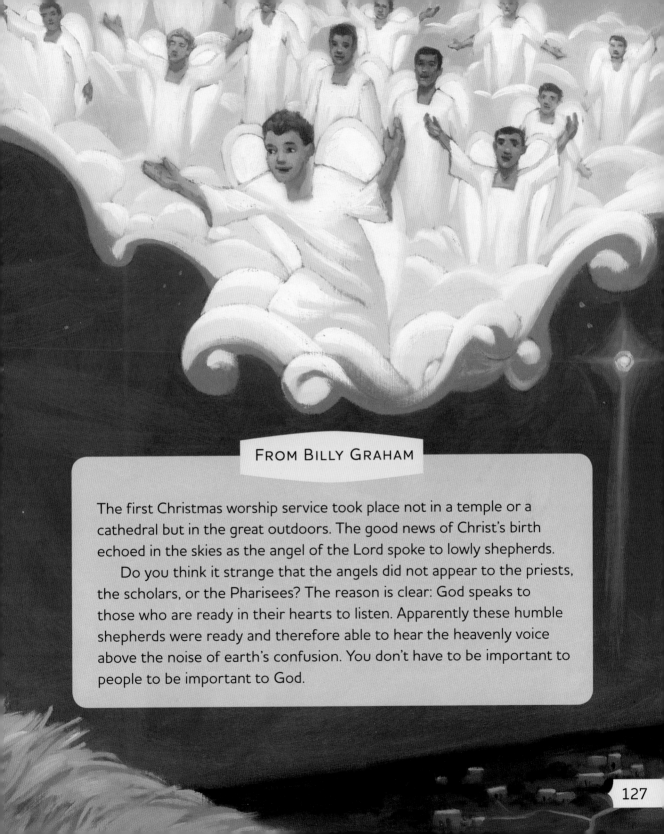

The first Christmas worship service took place not in a temple or a cathedral but in the great outdoors. The good news of Christ's birth echoed in the skies as the angel of the Lord spoke to lowly shepherds.

Do you think it strange that the angels did not appear to the priests, the scholars, or the Pharisees? The reason is clear: God speaks to those who are ready in their hearts to listen. Apparently these humble shepherds were ready and therefore able to hear the heavenly voice above the noise of earth's confusion. You don't have to be important to people to be important to God.

A Visit from the Wise Men

Selected Scripture from Matthew 2

After Jesus was born in Bethlehem in the days of Herod the king, behold, wise men from the East came to Jerusalem, saying, "Where is He who has been born King of the Jews? For we have seen His star in the East and have come to worship Him."

King Herod was troubled that another king had been born. Herod sent the wise men to Bethlehem, telling them to return with word about exactly where this new king was. Herod said he also wanted to worship the king, but he really wanted to destroy Him.

The star [the wise men] had seen in the East went before them, till it came and stood over where the young Child was. When they saw the star, they rejoiced with exceedingly great joy. And when they had come into the house, they saw the young Child with Mary His mother, and fell down and worshiped Him. And they presented gifts to Him: gold, frankincense, and myrrh.

Warned in a dream that they should not return to Herod, they departed for their own country another way.

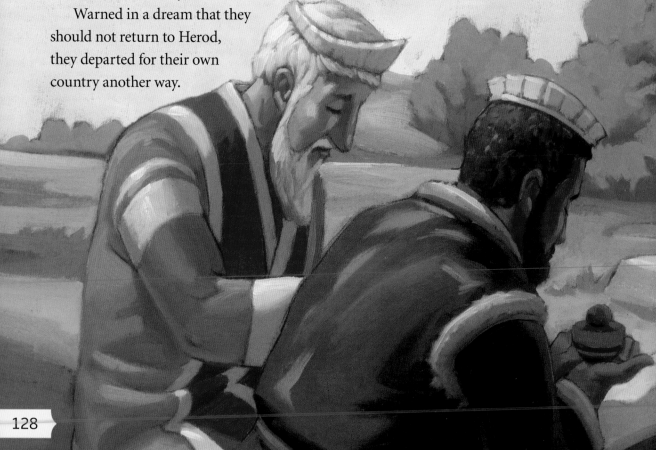

Jesus came into the world to save all kinds of people: rich and poor, black and white, educated and illiterate, sophisticated and ordinary—and anyone in between.

Yet only two groups of people gathered to honor Jesus when He was born. One was the shepherds—lowly, at the bottom of the social ladder, uneducated, unsophisticated. The other group was the wise men—intellectual, from another race and country, wealthy, respected. They could hardly have been more different!

By bringing both groups to see Jesus—one by an angelic announcement, one by the appearance of a miraculous star—God was telling us that Jesus is the Savior for everyone.

Boy Jesus in the Temple

Selected Scripture from Luke 2

[Jesus] grew and became strong in spirit, filled with wisdom; and the grace of God was upon Him.

When Jesus was twelve, his family and many friends went to Jerusalem to celebrate Passover as they did every year. On the return trip, Mary and Joseph thought Jesus was with friends or family, but at the end of the first day of traveling, they couldn't find Him when they looked for Him. Mary and Joseph went back to Jerusalem.

After three days they found Him in the temple, sitting in the midst of the teachers, both listening to them and asking them questions. All who heard Him were astonished at His understanding and answers. [Mary and Joseph] were amazed; and His mother said, "Son, why have You done this to us? Your father and I have sought You anxiously."

He said, "Why did you seek Me? Did you not know that I must be about My Father's business?"

The family then returned to Nazareth.

And Jesus increased in wisdom and stature, and in favor with God and men.

If Jesus found it important to be in God's house learning more about God's Word, shouldn't we as well? God wants us to grow in our faith, and one of the ways we can do this is by spending time and worshiping with other believers.

Jesus said He had to "be about [His] Father's business," and we should be too. God can use the preaching of His Word and time spent with other Christians to help you do that and make you more like Christ.

Jesus Is Baptized

Selected Scripture from Matthew 3

John the Baptist came preaching in the wilderness of Judea, and saying, "Repent, for the kingdom of heaven is at hand!"

John was clothed in camel's hair, with a leather belt around his waist; and his food was locusts and wild honey.

People came from faraway places to see John, confess their sins, and be baptized.

When he saw many Pharisees and Sadducees coming to his baptism, he said, "I baptize you with water unto repentance, but He who is coming after me is mightier than I, whose sandals I am not worthy to carry. He will baptize you with the Holy Spirit and fire."

John was surprised when Jesus came to him to be baptized.

John tried to prevent Him, saying, "I need to be baptized by You, and are You coming to me?"

Jesus insisted, reminding John that the prophets had said this must happen.

When He had been baptized, Jesus came up immediately from the water; and behold, the heavens were opened to Him, and He saw the Spirit of God descending like a dove and alighting upon Him. Suddenly a voice came from heaven, saying, "This is My beloved Son, in whom I am well pleased."

All along, John's job was to prepare people to meet Jesus. So when Jesus came to John, John told the crowd to follow Jesus and put Him first. John said, "He must increase, but I must decrease" (John 3:30).

Jesus alone was the Son of God, sent from heaven as God's final sacrifice for our sins. He later told His disciples, "You believe in God, believe also in Me" (John 14:1). If we believe in what God made and what God said, we will believe in the One God sent.

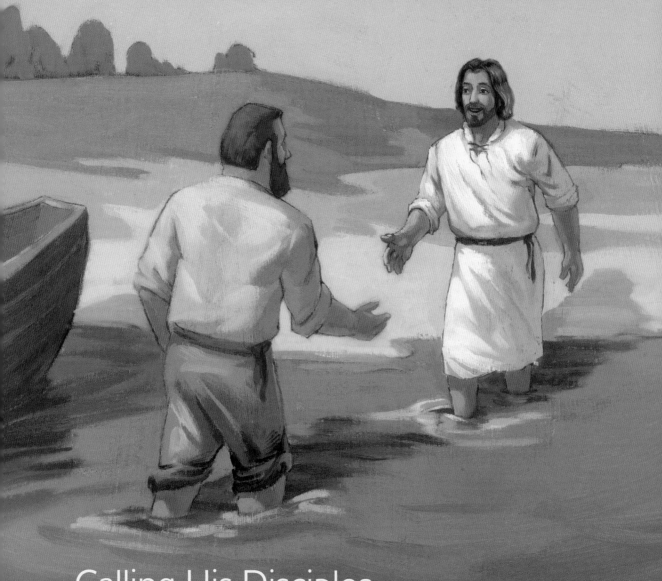

Calling His Disciples

Selected Scripture from Matthew 4, 9, and 11

Jesus began to preach and to say, "Repent, for the kingdom of heaven is at hand."

Jesus, walking by the Sea of Galilee, saw two brothers, Simon called Peter, and Andrew his brother, casting a net into the sea; for they were fishermen. He said to them, "Follow Me, and I will make you fishers of men." They immediately left their nets and followed Him.

Going on, [Jesus] saw James and John his brother, in the boat with their father, mending their nets. He called them, and immediately they left the boat and their father, and followed Him.

[Jesus] saw a man named Matthew sitting at the tax office. And He said to him, "Follow Me." So he arose and followed Him.

[At a later time] Jesus said, "Take My yoke upon you and learn from Me, for I am gentle and lowly in heart, and you will find rest for your souls."

Do you know what it means to be a disciple? A disciple is a learner.

A disciple must spend time with his teacher in order to gain wisdom, knowledge, and understanding. He knows he cannot get it any other way. It would be like trying to graduate from college without ever attending classes. It is impossible to do.

All of us who belong to Christ are His disciples. We cannot spend time with Jesus in person like the first disciples did. But we can hear Him speak and learn from Him just the same by reading what He said when He was here, by speaking to Him through prayer, and by obeying His teachings.

Jesus said that he who keeps God's commandments is the one who truly loves God.

Sermon on the Mount

Selected Scripture from Matthew 5–7

Jesus went throughout Galilee teaching in synagogues, preaching the gospel, and healing people. Great crowds started following Him and heard teachings like these:

"You have heard that it was said, 'You shall love your neighbor and hate your enemy.' But I say to you, love your enemies, do good to those who hate you.

"Do a charitable deed in secret; and your Father who sees in secret will Himself reward you.

"When you pray, you shall not be like the hypocrites. They love to pray standing in the synagogues and on the corners of the streets, that they may be seen by men. When you pray, go into your room, and when you have shut your door, pray to your Father who is in the secret place; and your Father who sees in secret will reward you openly.

"If you forgive men their trespasses, your heavenly Father will also forgive you. But if you do not forgive men their trespasses, neither will your Father forgive your trespasses.

"Whatever you want men to do to you, do also to them."

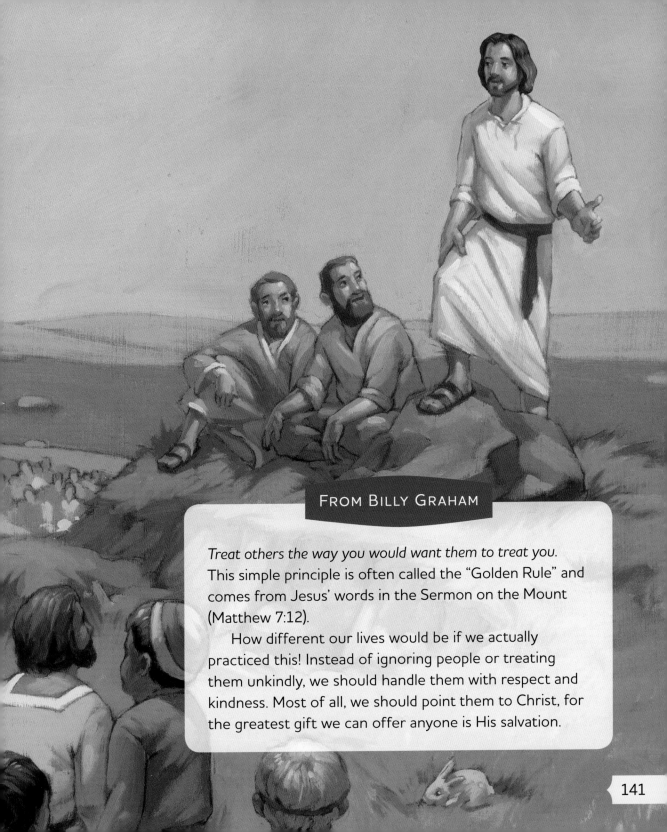

Treat others the way you would want them to treat you.
This simple principle is often called the "Golden Rule" and comes from Jesus' words in the Sermon on the Mount (Matthew 7:12).

How different our lives would be if we actually practiced this! Instead of ignoring people or treating them unkindly, we should handle them with respect and kindness. Most of all, we should point them to Christ, for the greatest gift we can offer anyone is His salvation.

Zacchaeus:
A Wee Little Man

Selected Scripture from Luke 19

Jesus entered and passed through Jericho. There was a man named Zacchaeus who was a chief tax collector, and he was rich. He sought to see who Jesus was, but could not because of the crowd, for he was of short stature. So he ran ahead and climbed up into a sycamore tree to see Him.

When Jesus came to the place, He looked up and saw him, and said to him, "Zacchaeus, make haste and come down, for today I must stay at your house." So [Zacchaeus] made haste and came down, and received [Jesus] joyfully. But when [the crowd] saw it, they all complained, saying, "He has gone to be a guest with a man who is a sinner."

Then Zacchaeus said to the Lord, "Look, Lord, I give half of my goods to the poor; and if I have taken anything from anyone by false accusation, I restore fourfold."

And Jesus said to him, "Today salvation has come to this house for the Son of Man has come to seek and to save that which was lost."

FROM BILLY GRAHAM

The Bible is full of people from all walks of life who have been changed by getting to know Jesus Christ. Zacchaeus, a tax collector, and not a very honest one at that, was in the habit of cheating people out of money, but when he met Jesus, all that changed. He repented and wanted to obey God.

Before meeting Jesus, Zacchaeus was not only dishonest but also lonely. He was hated and avoided by everyone. If Jesus had followed the crowd, He would have avoided Zacchaeus altogether. But Jesus paid no attention to what everyone else thought. He made a point to reach out to Zacchaeus. Everyone—including people who are left out or avoided—needs Jesus.

No Worries!

Selected Scripture from Matthew 6

"Do not worry about your life, what you will eat or what you will drink; nor about your body, what you will put on. Look at the birds of the air, for they neither sow nor reap nor gather into barns; yet your heavenly Father feeds them. Are you not of more value than they?

"Why do you worry about clothing? Consider the lilies of the field, how they grow: they neither toil nor spin. Now if God so clothes the grass of the field, will He not much more clothe you?

"Do not worry, saying, 'What shall we eat?' or 'What shall we drink?' or 'What shall we wear?' Your heavenly Father knows that you need all these things. But seek first the kingdom of God and His righteousness, and all these things shall be added to you."

Most of us are pretty good at worrying, aren't we?

But when worries come, it is helpful to think about the Bible's promises. God loves you, and He will never leave you. Jesus showed God's love for us by giving His life so that we could live forever with Him in heaven.

Does this mean that things will never go wrong or that we'll never have any problems? Absolutely not! But it does mean that nothing we experience catches God by surprise or is too big for Him to handle. God will never allow anything to come your way that is too much for you.

Thank God every day for the blessings you have. Worries go away when we are grateful. When problems do come, give them to God. Since God takes care of the smallest birds, can't we trust Him to take care of us?

Jesus Heals the Centurion's Servant

Selected Scripture from Matthew 8

Now when Jesus had entered Capernaum, a centurion [a Roman army officer] came to Him, pleading with Him, saying, "Lord, my servant is lying at home paralyzed, dreadfully tormented."

And Jesus said to him, "I will come and heal him."

The centurion answered and said, "Lord, I am not worthy that You should come under my roof. But only speak a word, and my servant will be healed. For I also am a man under authority, having soldiers under me. And I say to this one, 'Go,' and he goes; and to another, 'Come,' and he comes; and to my servant, 'Do this,' and he does it."

When Jesus heard it, He marveled, and said to those who followed, "Assuredly, I say to you, I have not found such great faith, not even in Israel!" Then Jesus said to the centurion, "Go your way; and as you have believed, so let it be done for you." And his servant was healed that same hour.

FROM BILLY GRAHAM

The centurion had many good qualities, but Jesus especially noticed his faith—He marveled at it. The greatest way we can please God is to believe His Word and have complete confidence in His character, in who He is. How big do you think God is? If God is limited—if He isn't all-powerful and all-knowing—then we would be right to doubt that He could bring good things into our lives. But God isn't limited! He isn't like a computer without enough memory. There is no end to God's knowledge and wisdom, or to His goodness and power. Have complete confidence in your great God!

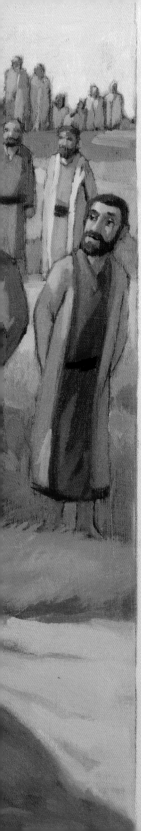

Feeding Five Thousand

Selected Scripture from John 6

Jesus had been teaching a large crowd, and soon it was time for dinner. Jesus told the disciples to feed them, but the disciples said they didn't know how they could—they didn't have enough money to buy all of them food.

One of His disciples, Andrew, Simon Peter's brother, said to Him, "There is a lad here who has five barley loaves and two small fish, but what are they among so many?"

Then Jesus said, "Make the people sit down." Now there was much grass in the place. So the men sat down, in number about five thousand. And Jesus took the loaves, and when He had given thanks He distributed them to the disciples, and the disciples to those sitting down; and likewise of the fish, as much as they wanted. So when they were filled, He said to His disciples, "Gather up the fragments that remain, so that nothing is lost." Therefore they gathered them up, and filled twelve baskets with the fragments of the five barley loaves which were left over by those who had eaten.

FROM BILLY GRAHAM

The disciples could not have known what Jesus would do with only five loaves and two fish. The Bible tells us that everyone in the crowd ate until they were full—and the men alone numbered five thousand.

Jesus only had a small amount of food, but in His hands God multiplied it, and it became a huge feast for the crowd. In the same way, God is able to take what little things we have, like our talents or trust, and use them to accomplish His purposes—if we dedicate them to Him.

Walking on Water

Selected Scripture from Matthew 14

The disciples went into the boat while Jesus spent time alone in prayer.

In the night Jesus went to them, walking on the sea. When the disciples saw Him, they were troubled, saying, "It is a ghost!" And they cried out for fear.

Immediately Jesus spoke, saying, "Be of good cheer! It is I; do not be afraid."

Peter said, "Lord, if it is You, command me to come to You on the water."

He said, "Come." When Peter had come down out of the boat, he walked on the water to go to Jesus. But when [Peter] saw that the wind was boisterous, he was afraid; and beginning to sink he cried out, saying, "Lord, save me!"

Immediately Jesus stretched out His hand and caught [Peter], and said, "Why did you doubt?" When they got into the boat, the wind ceased.

Those in the boat came and worshiped [Jesus], saying, "Truly You are the Son of God."

From Billy Graham

Jesus lived in a small country and never went beyond its borders. He was so poor that He said He had nowhere to lay His head. He rode on another man's donkey. He crossed the lake in another man's boat. He was buried in another man's grave.

He never wrote a book. Yet if all the words that have been written about Him were brought together, they would fill a thousand libraries.

He never founded a college. Yet His teachings have lasted for more than two thousand years.

He never carried a sword or organized an army. Yet He founded an empire, and millions today would die for Him.

As the disciples said, truly He is the Son of God. Praise His name!

Jesus' Story of the Prodigal Son

Selected Scripture from Luke 15

[Jesus] said: "A certain man had two sons. The younger of them said to his father, 'Father, give me the portion of goods that falls to me.' So [the father] divided to them his livelihood. And not many days after, the younger son gathered all together, journeyed to a far country, and there wasted his possessions. But when he had spent all, there arose a severe famine in that land, and he began to be in want. He went and [worked] to feed swine. He would gladly have filled his stomach with the pods that the swine ate, and no one gave him anything.

"But when he came to himself, he said, 'How many of my father's hired servants have bread enough and to spare, and I perish with hunger! I will arise and go to my father, and will say to him, "Father, I have sinned against heaven and before you, and I am no longer worthy to be called your son. Make me like one of your hired servants."'

"And he arose and came to his father. But when he was still a great way off, his father saw him and had compassion, and ran and fell on his neck and kissed him. The son said to him, 'Father, I have sinned against heaven and in your sight, and am no longer worthy to be called your son.'

"But the father said to his servants, 'Bring out the best robe and put it on him. And bring the fatted calf here and kill it, and let us eat and be merry; for this my son was lost and is found.' And they began to be merry."

FROM BILLY GRAHAM

The story of the prodigal son shows God's desire for human fellowship. He hurts over His children who have wandered far from Him and longs for them to come home and be near to Him.

All through the Bible we see God's patience and perseverance as He pursues stubborn people—people who were born to be His sons and daughters but who chose not to follow Him. From Genesis to Revelation, God is constantly saying to people, "Return to Me, and I will return to you."

Incredible as it may seem, God wants us to be close with Him. He wants to be a father to us, to shield us, to protect us, to counsel us, and to guide us in our way through life.

A Blessing for the Children

Selected Scripture from Mark 10

Then they brought little children to Him, that He might touch them; but the disciples rebuked those who brought them. But when Jesus saw it, He was greatly displeased and said to them, "Let the little children come to Me, and do not forbid them; for of such is the kingdom of God. Assuredly, I say to you, whoever does not receive the kingdom of God as a little child will by no means enter it." And He took them up in His arms, laid His hands on them, and blessed them.

FROM BILLY GRAHAM

Jesus welcomed the children who flocked around Him. He told the disciples not to keep the little ones from coming to Him, because God's kingdom is full of people who are like them (Matthew 19:14). Their openness, their enthusiasm, their trust—all these delighted Jesus, just like He delights in you! No matter how old we grow, God wants our faith to be like that of little children.

157

The Widow's Coins

Selected Scripture from Luke 21

[Jesus] looked up and saw the rich putting their gifts into the treasury, and He saw also a certain poor widow putting in two mites. So He said, "Truly I say to you that this poor widow has put in more than all; for all these out of their abundance have put in offerings for God, but she out of her poverty put in all the livelihood that she had."

Two things happen when we give. First, God wants to help us have the attitude that what we have is not really ours. Everything we have belongs to God.

Second, when we give, we meet the needs of other people whom God also loves. By giving to others we show God's love for them. So giving becomes not only a way people's needs are met but also a way we tell people about God's love and His greatest gift, His Son, the Lord Jesus Christ.

Entering Jerusalem

Selected Scripture from Matthew 21

Now when they drew near Jerusalem, Jesus sent two disciples, saying, "Go into the village, and immediately you will find a donkey tied, and a colt with her. Loose them and bring them to Me."

So the disciples went and did as Jesus commanded them. They brought the donkey and the colt, laid their clothes on them, and set Him on them. And a very great multitude spread their clothes on the road; others cut down branches from the trees and spread them on the road. Then the multitudes cried out, saying:

> "Hosanna to the Son of David!
> 'Blessed is He who comes in the name of the Lord!'
> Hosanna in the highest!"

And when He had come into Jerusalem, all the city was moved, saying, "Who is this?"

So the multitudes said, "This is Jesus, the prophet from Nazareth of Galilee."

FROM BILLY GRAHAM

While the people were shouting, "Hosanna!" Jesus knew it would not be long before they would be shouting, "Crucify Him!" He could have turned back, but instead He kept moving forward—toward the cross.

Jesus came into the world so that we might know that God loves us, and that we were made to know and love Him. He came to bridge the gap that separated us from our Creator.

Every time Jesus fed the hungry, it was as if He were saying, "I love you and want to take care of you." Every time He healed someone, it was like He was saying, "It hurts Me to see you in pain, and I want to help you." Everything He did—including choosing the cross—showed that He came to bring us closer to our loving Father in heaven.

161

When Jesus' disciples asked Him where they should prepare for the Passover (an annual Jewish festival commemorating God's deliverance of His people from their slavery in Egypt), He gave them specific instructions.

So His disciples went into the city, and found it just as He had said to them; and they prepared the Passover.

In the evening He came with the twelve. Now as they sat and ate, Jesus said, "One of you who eats with Me will betray Me."

And they began to be sorrowful, and to say to Him one by one, "Is it I?" And another said, "Is it I?"

He answered and said to them, "It is one of the twelve, who dips with Me in the dish."

As they were eating, Jesus took bread, blessed and broke it, and gave it to them and said, "Take, eat; this is My body."

Then He took the cup, and when He had given thanks He gave it to them, and they all drank from it. And He said to them, "This is My blood of the new covenant, which is shed for many."

When they had sung a hymn, they went out to the Mount of Olives.

As communion was being held in a church in Scotland one day, the bread and the cup came to a sixteen-year-old girl. She hesitated, thinking she couldn't receive it. But John Duncan, a famous theologian, reached over, touched her shoulder, and said tenderly, "Take it, lassie; it's for sinners!"

Communion is all about the cross. In the Lord's Supper, Jesus likens Himself to the lamb that was offered in the sacrifice of atonement and says to His disciples and to all who will believe in Him, "This is My body broken for you." This is symbolic of what He did on the cross. When the cup is offered, the emphasis is upon the fact that His blood is shed for the remission of sins. The bread and the cup remind us how Jesus' death on the cross—His body and His blood—make it possible for us to be forgiven. We can touch them, taste them, and see them. We have the bread and the cup in our hands, but we have Christ, and the forgiveness He brings, in our hearts.

Praying in the Garden

Selected Scripture from Mark 14

Then [Jesus and the eleven disciples] came to Gethsemane; and He said, "Sit here while I pray." He took Peter, James, and John with Him, and He began to be troubled and deeply distressed. Then He said to them, "My soul is exceedingly sorrowful, even to death. Stay here and watch."

He went a little farther, and fell on the ground, and prayed. "Abba, Father, all things are possible for You. Take this cup away from Me; nevertheless, not what I will, but what You will."

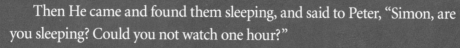

Then He came and found them sleeping, and said to Peter, "Simon, are you sleeping? Could you not watch one hour?"

Again He went away and prayed, and spoke the same words. And when He returned, He found them asleep again, for their eyes were heavy; and they did not know what to answer Him.

Then He came the third time and said to them, "Are you still sleeping and resting? It is enough! The hour has come."

From Billy Graham

Jesus' prayer in the garden may be the most amazing prayer of all time. First He asked that He would not have to go through the suffering of the cross. But then, in the very next breath He said, "Nevertheless not My will, but Yours, be done." What a prayer! What strength! What power!

God wants to be with us as we face hard things. Turn to Him when you need help—just like Jesus did. He may not make your problems go away, but He will help you deal with them and overcome them in His strength.

God also knows our heart and our true desires, and He knows what is best for us. That is why we should always pray for what God wants and not only what we want—just like Jesus did. We need to ask God to change our hearts so that more than anything, we want what God wants for our lives.

Jesus Is Arrested

Selected Scripture from Mark 14 and John 18

[Then Jesus said to His disciples], "The Son of Man is being betrayed into the hands of sinners. Rise, let us be going. See, My betrayer is at hand."

Judas, who betrayed [Jesus], knew the place; for Jesus often met there with His disciples. Then Judas, having received a detachment of troops, and officers from the chief priests and Pharisees, came there with lanterns, torches, and weapons. Jesus therefore, knowing all things that would come upon Him, went forward and said to them, "Whom are you seeking?"

They answered Him, "Jesus of Nazareth."

Jesus said to them, "I am He. If you seek Me, let these go their way."

Then the detachment of troops and the captain and the officers of the Jews arrested Jesus and bound Him.

FROM BILLY GRAHAM

In the garden as Jesus wrestled over what He was about to do, no angel could protect Him from it or relieve His suffering. It was His and His alone. The Savior accepted His sacrifice and took upon Himself the guilt of us all. The angels would have helped Him in that hour, but Christ did not call for their help. This One who said no to angel help said, in effect, "I will die for the sins of people because I love them so much."

Before Pilate

Selected Scripture from Luke 23

Jesus was brought before the chief priests, elders, and scribes. When Jesus said He was the Son of God, they all said He had committed a serious sin. They wanted Him to be executed, but the Roman governor, Pontius Pilate, would decide what would happen.

Then the multitude led [Jesus] to Pilate.

Pilate asked Him, "Are You the King of the Jews?"

[Jesus] said, "It is as you say."

Then Pilate, when he had called together the chief priests, the rulers, and the people, said to them, "I have found no fault in this Man; indeed nothing deserving of death has been done by Him."

And they all cried out at once, "Away with this Man. Crucify Him, crucify Him!"

They were insistent, demanding with loud voices that He be crucified. And [Pilate] delivered Jesus to their will.

The name of Pontius Pilate will stand forever as an example of someone who knew what was right—but failed to do it. Repeatedly he told the mob demanding Jesus' death that he found no basis for condemning Him—but in the end, Pilate caved in to the pressures of the crowd and ordered His death. Publicly Pilate told the crowd that they alone were responsible for Jesus' death (Matthew 27:24), but in reality Pilate's cowardice also sent Jesus to the cross.

We all like to be liked—but that can be a very dangerous thing if we are seeking the approval of people instead of the approval of God. Make it your goal to live for Christ's approval and be faithful to Him, no matter what the crowd demands.

The Death of Jesus

Selected Scripture from Luke 23

Soldiers led Jesus to the hill where He and two criminals would be put to death. As He hung dying, Jesus asked God to forgive His murderers because, He said, they did not know what they were doing.

Now it was about the sixth hour, and there was darkness over all the earth until the ninth hour.

Jesus cried out with a loud voice, "Father, 'into Your hands I commit My spirit.'" Having said this, He breathed His last.

So when the centurion saw what had happened, he glorified God, saying, "Certainly this was a righteous Man!"

The whole crowd, seeing what had been done, beat their breasts and returned.

Now there was a man named Joseph, a good and just man. He was from Arimathea, a city of the Jews. This man went to Pilate and asked for the body of Jesus. Then he took it down, wrapped it in linen, and laid it in a tomb that was hewn out of the rock.

And the women who had come with [Jesus] from Galilee followed after, and they observed the tomb and how His body was laid.

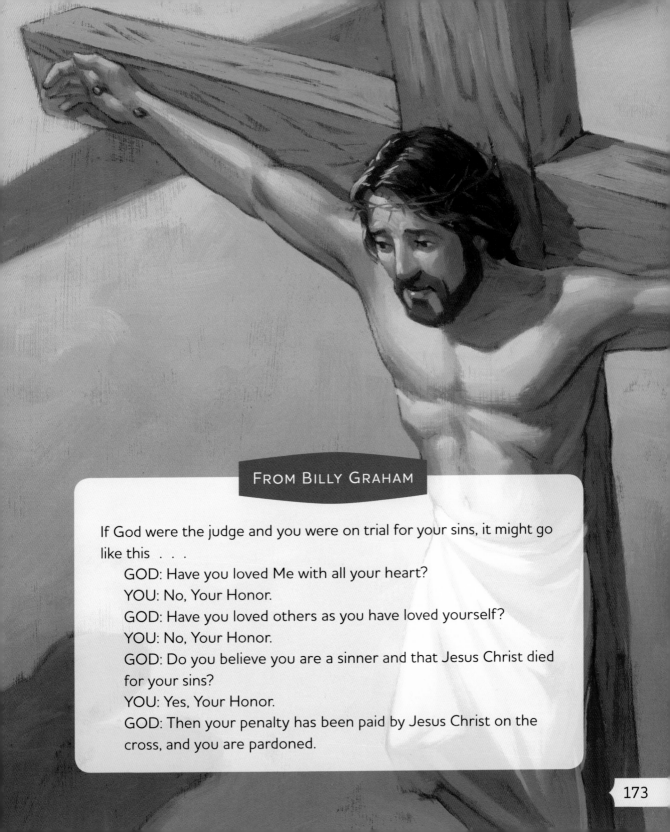

If God were the judge and you were on trial for your sins, it might go like this . . .

GOD: Have you loved Me with all your heart?

YOU: No, Your Honor.

GOD: Have you loved others as you have loved yourself?

YOU: No, Your Honor.

GOD: Do you believe you are a sinner and that Jesus Christ died for your sins?

YOU: Yes, Your Honor.

GOD: Then your penalty has been paid by Jesus Christ on the cross, and you are pardoned.

The women who had seen where Jesus was buried went to the tomb early in the morning.

They found the stone rolled away. Then they went in and did not find the body of the Lord Jesus. Two men stood by them in shining garments. Then, as they were afraid and bowed their faces to the earth, [the men] said, "Why do you seek the living among the dead? [Jesus] is not here, but is risen!"

Then [the women] returned from the tomb and told all these things to the eleven and to all the rest. Their words seemed like idle tales, and [the apostles] did not believe them. But Peter arose and ran to the tomb; and stooping down, he saw the linen cloths lying by themselves; and he departed, marveling to himself at what had happened.

On that first Easter morning, something happened that had never happened before in the history of the human race—and would never happen again: someone came back from the dead, never to die again.

The resurrection proved beyond all doubt that Jesus was the Son of God sent from heaven to save us from our sins. Because He rose from the dead, our salvation is secure.

But Jesus' resurrection also tells us that there is life beyond the grave. This world is not all there is; when we die, we continue to live—either with God in the place of endless joy the Bible calls heaven or without God in the place of utter darkness called hell.

Jesus has opened the way to heaven for us. Because Jesus rose from the dead, death has been defeated and heaven awaits us.

Jesus Returns to Heaven

Selected Scripture from John 20, Matthew 28, and Acts 1

At evening, when the doors were shut where the disciples were assembled, Jesus came and stood in the midst, and said to them, "Peace be with you." He showed them His hands and His side. The disciples were glad when they saw the [risen] Lord.

Then the eleven disciples went into Galilee, to the mountain which Jesus had appointed for them. When they saw Him, they worshiped Him.

Jesus spoke to them, saying, "Go and make disciples of all the nations, baptizing them in the name of the Father and of the Son and of the Holy Spirit, teaching them to observe all things that I have commanded you; and lo, I am with you always."

And He said to [His disciples], "You shall receive power when the Holy Spirit has come upon you; and you shall be witnesses to Me to the end of the earth."

When He had spoken these things, while they watched, He was taken up, and a cloud received Him out of their sight.

FROM BILLY GRAHAM

Satan's power and the strength of sin's hold over us are real . . . but *by His death and resurrection, Christ defeated Satan and sin!* Satan had done his worst, and during those dark hours when Jesus hung on the cross, it looked as if Satan had won. But he hadn't! Christ beat death by His resurrection—the proof was right before the disciples' eyes as Jesus showed them His hands and side. He had won over all the forces of evil and death and hell.

And so Jesus told His followers to spread the message of His victory and "make disciples of all the nations" (Matthew 28:19). Tell anyone who hasn't heard the good news—Satan has been defeated, and Christ is the victor!

The Gift of the Holy Spirit

Selected Scripture from Acts 2

When the Day of Pentecost had fully come, [the disciples] were all in one place. Suddenly there came a sound from heaven, as of a rushing mighty wind, and it filled the whole house where they were sitting. Then there appeared to them divided tongues, as of fire, and one sat upon each of them. They were all filled with the Holy Spirit and began to speak [in] other [languages].

There were dwelling in Jerusalem Jews, devout men, from every nation under heaven. And when this sound occurred, they were all amazed and marveled, saying, "Look, are not all these who speak Galileans? How is it that we hear our own language?"

Peter, standing up with the eleven, said, "Men of Israel: Jesus of Nazareth, a Man attested by God to you by miracles which God did through Him in your midst—Him you have crucified and put to death; God raised [Him] up, having loosed the pains of death. God has made this Jesus, whom you crucified, both Lord and Christ."

When they heard this, they were cut to the heart.

Peter said, "Repent, and be baptized in the name of Jesus Christ; and you shall receive the gift of the Holy Spirit."

Then those who gladly received his word were baptized; and that day about three thousand souls were added to them.

FROM BILLY GRAHAM

Pentecost was a special time of year for the Jews, and this particular Pentecost was the time when God first gave the gift of the Holy Spirit. Ever since then, the Holy Spirit has lived in the hearts of all true believers.

The Holy Spirit helps us see our sin and guides us in the way we should live. He is the source of power who meets our needs and helps us when we are weak. He gives us the power to be truly good and to serve others.

To the great gift of forgiveness God adds the great gift of the Holy Spirit!

Peter and John Perform a Miracle

Selected Scripture from Acts 3–4

One day as Peter and John went to the temple, a man who had been crippled all his life asked them for money.

Peter said, "Silver and gold I do not have, but what I do have I give you: In the name of Jesus Christ of Nazareth, rise up and walk." And [Peter] took him by the right hand and lifted him up, and immediately his feet and ankle bones received strength.

So he, leaping up, stood and walked and entered the temple with them—walking, leaping, and praising God. All the people saw him walking and praising God. They were filled with wonder and amazement.

So Peter responded to the people: "Why do you marvel at this? The God of Abraham, Isaac, and Jacob, the God of our fathers, glorified His Servant Jesus. God raised [Him] from the dead, of which we are witnesses. And His name has made this man strong. God, having raised up His Servant Jesus, sent Him to bless you, in turning away every one of you from your [sins]."

Many of those who heard the word believed; and the number of the men came to be about five thousand.

Peter, the weak, was transformed to Peter, the rock. All of the disciples were changed from ordinary individuals into special servants of God. Their faith and zeal were like a fire of belief in Jesus, which spread throughout Asia Minor, Europe, and the entire world. The world today still feels the powerful impact and influence of this little band of dedicated men.

Stephen's Faith

Selected Scripture from Acts 6–7

Stephen, full of faith and power, did great wonders and signs among the people.

People were jealous of Stephen, and they didn't know what to say against his arguments that Jesus was God's Son. So they found men to lie about Stephen, saying, "We have heard him speak against Moses and God" (Acts 6:11).

All who sat in the council, looking steadfastly at [Stephen], saw his face as the face of an angel.

[Stephen] said, "Which of the prophets did your fathers not persecute? And they killed those who foretold the coming of [Jesus], of whom you now have become the betrayers and murderers."

When [the council] heard these things, they gnashed their teeth. But [Stephen], being full of the Holy Spirit, gazed into heaven and saw the glory of God, and Jesus standing at the right hand of God, and said, "Look! I see the heavens opened and the Son of Man standing at the right hand of God!"

They stoned Stephen as he was saying, "Lord Jesus, receive my spirit." Then he knelt down and cried out with a loud voice, "Lord, do not charge them with this sin." And he fell asleep.

FROM BILLY GRAHAM

The Bible teaches that God does not always deliver His people from hard times. God has not promised to deliver us *from* trouble, but He has promised to go *with us through* the trouble.

Stephen was a young man who had a strong faith in God and was filled with the Holy Spirit (Acts 6:5). Enemies of Jesus stoned him to death, but Stephen had a joyous entry into heaven. Stay close to God, and when troubles come, you will have the strength to stand up for Christ. Keep depending on Him—He has promised to go with you every step of the way.

Philip's Conversation with the Traveler

Selected Scripture from Acts 8

An angel told Philip to leave Jerusalem and walk toward Gaza. When Philip obeyed, the Spirit then directed him to go to a certain chariot where an Ethiopian man was reading the writings of the prophet Isaiah.

Philip ran to him, and said, "Do you understand what you are reading?"

"How can I, unless someone guides me?"

Then Philip opened his mouth and preached Jesus to him. Now as they went down the road, they came to some water. And the [man] said, "See, here is water. What hinders me from being baptized?"

Philip said, "If you believe with all your heart, you may."

And he said, "I believe that Jesus Christ is the Son of God."

So he commanded the chariot to stand still. And both Philip and the [man] went down into the water, and [Philip] baptized him. When they came up out of the water, the Spirit of the Lord caught Philip away, so that the [man] saw him no more; and he went on his way rejoicing.

Jesus died to save people from even the farthest corners of the world—people you and I will never know during our lifetimes, but people we will be with in heaven forever. "For God so loved the world that He gave His only begotten Son" (John 3:16). God's salvation is offered to everyone in the world! No tribe or nation is beyond the reach of His love.

Jesus says we should help people from other places become His followers, just like Philip helped the Ethiopian man. You might do that someday by traveling to other countries, but you can also be part of God's grand design to bring people from every part of the world to Himself right where you are today. By praying, obeying God, being faithful, and serving others, you can have an impact for the gospel far beyond your homeland.

Saul Becomes a Believer

Selected Scripture from Acts 9

Saul's mission in life was to destroy anyone who followed Jesus.

As he journeyed near Damascus, suddenly a light shone around him from heaven. He fell to the ground, and heard a voice saying, "Saul, Saul, why are you persecuting Me?"

He said, "Who are You, Lord?"

The Lord said, "I am Jesus, whom you are persecuting."

Saul arose from the ground, and when his eyes were opened he saw no one. But [the men who journeyed with him] led him by the hand into Damascus. And he was three days without sight, and neither ate nor drank.

God sent a man named Ananias to Saul. When Ananias spoke, Saul could see again. After Ananias baptized him, Saul stayed in Jerusalem with Jesus' disciples.

And he spoke boldly in the name of the Lord Jesus.

FROM BILLY GRAHAM

When we first glimpse the apostle Paul in the Bible, he was called Saul—and his mission in life was to stamp out the Christian faith. But all that changed when he met the risen Lord Jesus Christ on the road to Damascus. Paul went from being someone who hurt the Christian faith to someone who fearlessly preached about Jesus throughout the Roman Empire.

What made him change? First, he became absolutely convinced that the gospel was true. Jesus Christ was the risen Son of God, sent from heaven to save us from our sins. How could Paul remain silent about this great truth?

Second, Paul began to see people the way God sees them. He now saw them as lost and confused—and as people for whom Christ died. What difference does the truth of the gospel make to you? Are you asking God to help you see others through His eyes?

The Angel's Assignment for Peter

Selected Scripture from Acts 10

An angel appeared to a godly man named Cornelius and told him to send men to Joppa to get Simon Peter. The next day when Peter was praying, God taught him that, unlike those who followed strict Jewish laws, people who followed Jesus could eat any food they wanted. As Peter was thinking about this new teaching, Cornelius's men arrived.

The Spirit said to [Peter], "Three men are seeking you. Go with them, doubting nothing; for I have sent them."

On the next day Peter went away with them.

Now Cornelius was waiting for them, and had called together his relatives and close friends. Peter said to them, "You know how unlawful it is for a Jewish man to keep company with one of another nation. But God has shown me that I should not call any man unclean. Whoever believes in [Jesus] will receive remission of sins."

The Holy Spirit fell upon the Gentiles also. And [Peter] commanded [those in Cornelius's household] to be baptized in the name of the Lord.

Peter and Cornelius were very different from each other, but the Bible makes it clear that God created everyone. Jesus loves all kinds of people from every single place in the world (Revelation 5:9). So when we don't love people because they are different from us, that is a sin in the eyes of God. And that kind of sin can lead to hatred and anger and fighting. None of those are pleasing to God. When we turn these feelings over to God, He can replace them with His love.

Godly and Gracious Lydia

Selected Scripture from Acts 16

Paul and Luke were in Philippi sharing the good news about Jesus.

On the Sabbath day [they] went out of the city to the riverside, where prayer was customarily made; and [they] sat down and spoke to the women who met there. Now a certain woman named Lydia heard [them]. She was a seller of purple [cloth] from the city of Thyatira, who worshiped God. The Lord opened her heart to heed the things spoken by Paul. When she and her household were baptized, she begged [them], saying, "If you have judged me to be faithful to the Lord, come to my house and stay." So she persuaded [them].

After a while Paul and Silas left, but they later returned to that area. They stayed at Lydia's house again and spent time with Christians who needed their encouragement.

FROM BILLY GRAHAM

Generosity means being willing to share what you have and give good things to others. It doesn't come naturally to most of us—not the kind of generosity the Bible wants us to have. Most of us will gladly give if we think the cause is worthy and we feel we can afford it. But the Bible urges us to give to God's work even when it's not easy to give. Generous Lydia opened her heart to Christ and her home to others.

Everything you have has been given to you by God. Put Christ first in everything, because Christ gave His all for you. You can be like Lydia, who was willing to give what she had to help others.

Paul and Silas in Prison

Selected Scripture from Acts 16

Paul cast an evil spirit out of a girl who made her owners a lot of money because of her fortune-telling. The angry owners had Paul and Silas arrested and put in prison. While they were there, something amazing happened.

At midnight Paul and Silas were praying and singing hymns to God, and the prisoners were listening to them. Suddenly there was a great earthquake; and immediately all the doors were opened and everyone's chains were loosed.

Then [the keeper of the prison] ran in, and fell down trembling before Paul and Silas. "Sirs, what must I do to be saved?"

So they said, "Believe on the Lord Jesus Christ, and you will be saved, you and your household." And he and all his family were baptized. Now when he had brought them into his house, he set food before them; and he rejoiced, having believed in God with all his household.

FROM BILLY GRAHAM

Paul and Silas had so much joy they were able to sing hymns and praises to God—even when they were in prison. Joy is produced in our hearts when we know that God loves us and when we have a close relationship with Him—by reading His Word, praying, desiring to honor Him in all that we do, and serving others.

Joy does not mean that we are never sad, that we never cry, or that we never get scared. The Bible says that when we face troubles, God will help us carry on and keep loving Him. Because He is with us, we can be "persecuted, but not forsaken; struck down, but not destroyed" (2 Corinthians 4:9). Paul and Silas had joy—and you can too.

197

Shipwreck!

Selected Scripture from Acts 27

Paul continued to be imprisoned for telling people about Jesus. He was sent to Rome to go on trial before Caesar. He warned his captors that it was too late in the season to set sail, but they did not listen. They sailed into a terrible storm. Paul said:

"Men, you should have listened to me, and not have sailed from Crete and incurred this disaster and loss. And now I urge you to take heart, for there will be no loss of life among you, but only of the ship. For there stood by me this night an angel of the God to whom I belong and whom I serve, saying, 'Do not be afraid, Paul; you must be brought before Caesar; and indeed God has granted you all those who sail with you.'"

The soldiers' plan was to kill the prisoners. But [a] centurion, wanting to save Paul, kept them from their purpose, and commanded that those who could swim should jump overboard first and get to land, and the rest, some on boards and some on parts of the ship. And so it was that they all escaped safely to land.

Even during a dangerous storm, Paul had peace and trusted God. How can we have this kind of peace? Before Jesus went to the cross, He promised His disciples He would give them His peace. He told them not to let their hearts be troubled or afraid (John 14:27). Jesus wants the same for us today too.

We are never alone if we know Christ. He loves us and is with us. He has told us that nothing will "be able to separate us from the love of God which is in Christ Jesus our Lord" (Romans 8:39). When life is hard, turn to Jesus, and you will find the peace, hope, and strength you need.

Paul's Letters from Prison

Selected Scripture from Philippians 4, 1 Corinthians 9, and 2 Timothy 4

Under the inspiration of the Holy Spirit, Paul wrote many letters that we believers read today. Here are thoughts from three of them.

Rejoice in the Lord always. Again I will say, rejoice!

Be anxious for nothing, but in everything by prayer and supplication, with thanksgiving, let your requests be made known to God; and the peace of God, which surpasses all understanding, will guard your hearts and minds through Christ Jesus.

Finally, brethren, whatever things are true, whatever things are noble, whatever things are just, whatever things are pure, whatever things are lovely, whatever things are of good report, if there is any virtue and if there is anything praiseworthy—meditate on these things.

Do you not know that those who run in a race all run, but one receives the prize? Run in such a way that you may obtain it.

I have fought the good fight, I have finished the race, I have kept the faith.

Like the marathon runner, we [Christians] run a long race. It lasts as long as we are alive, and we aren't meant to wander off the track, or quit and join the crowd on the sidelines, or slow down and take it easy.

Commitment for an athlete means having a strong desire to become the best he possibly can at his sport. He has one goal: to win. Commitment isn't just a hope or a wish. He uses all his strength to become the best.

Commitment must be coupled with *discipline* if an athlete is ever to achieve her goal. A lazy athlete will never become a successful athlete, no matter how talented she is.

As a "runner" in God's "race," Paul was both *committed* to the goal and *disciplined* to do whatever he needed to do to reach it. Are you committed and disciplined?

John's Message to the Churches

Selected Scripture from Revelation 4

The apostle John shared this vision from God when he wrote the book called Revelation.

I looked, and behold, a door standing open in heaven. And the voice I heard was like a trumpet, saying, "Come up here."

Immediately I [saw] a throne set in heaven, and One sat on the throne. There was a rainbow around the throne, in appearance like an emerald. Around the throne were twenty-four thrones, and on the thrones I saw twenty-four elders sitting, clothed in white robes; and they had crowns of gold on their heads. From the throne proceeded lightnings, thunderings, and voices. Before the throne there was a sea of glass, like crystal. And around the throne were four living creatures, saying:

> "Holy, holy, holy,
> Lord God Almighty,
> Who was and is and is to come!"

The living creatures give glory and honor and thanks to Him who sits on the throne, who lives forever and ever.

From Billy Graham

It's natural to wonder what heaven must be like. Are the streets really paved with gold? What will we do with our time? A hundred other questions crowd our minds—and the Bible doesn't answer all of them. Heaven is so amazing, and our understanding is so limited, that we can only barely imagine heaven's glory.

But these truths about heaven are absolutely clear: We will be safely in God's presence forever. All our fears and sadness and disappointments will be gone. We will be changed—for we will be like Christ!

Someday . . . Heaven!

Selected Scripture from Revelation 21–22

Now I saw a new heaven and a new earth, for the first heaven and the first earth had passed away. Then I, John, saw the holy city, New Jerusalem, coming down out of heaven from God. And I heard a loud voice from heaven saying, "Behold, the tabernacle of God is with men, and He will dwell with them, and they shall be His people. God Himself will be with them and be their God. And God will wipe away every tear from their eyes; there shall be no more death, nor sorrow, nor crying. There shall be no more pain, for the former things have passed away."

Then [Jesus] who sat on the throne said, "Behold, I make all things new."

The grace of our Lord Jesus Christ be with you all. Amen.

The description of heaven and the holy city found in Revelation 21 and 22 is beyond understanding. The Bible talks about gates of pearl, streets of gold, a river of life, and a tree of life.

The Bible teaches that heaven, God's house, will be a happy home because there will be nothing in it to keep us from being happy (Revelation 21:4).

Think of a place where there will be no sin, no sorrow, no arguments, no misunderstandings, no hurt feelings, no pain, no sickness, and no death. That is a peek of what it will be like in heaven!

A Prayer from Billy Graham

Dear God,

We thank You for every blessing we have received from You. We thank You for giving us Your good news—for showing us that You are a God of mercy and love. We are sinners, and we have disobeyed You. Yet when You could have turned us away, You offered us forgiveness and You invited us to become Your adopted children. Thank You, Father, for Your amazing love!

As we love You back day after day, remind us how much we need You. Help us to remember that there is right and wrong in this world and to seek Your kingdom before anything else. Remind us of Your love and forgiveness.

We ask that You would bless each precious child who reads this book. Guide them in knowing You and Your good future for them. Give them wisdom—as You have promised You will to those who ask—and strength You alone can give. Most of all, may each of them respond to You by turning in faith to Jesus Christ, and asking Him to come into their hearts and lives as their personal Lord and Savior.

We pray in the name of the Father and the Son and the Holy Spirit, amen.